THE
NICKEL
AND
DIME
DECADE

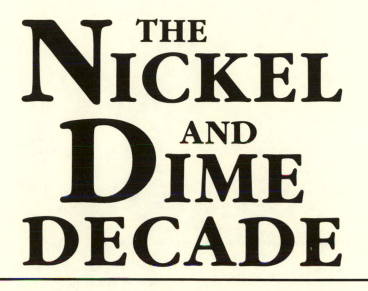

THE
NICKEL
AND
DIME
DECADE

*American Popular Culture
During the 1930s*

GARY DEAN BEST

Westport, Connecticut
London

973.9
B56n

Library of Congress Cataloging-in-Publication Data

Best, Gary Dean.
    The nickel and dime decade : American popular culture during the
1930s / Gary Dean Best.
        p. cm.
    Includes bibliographical references and index.
    ISBN 0-275-94395-X (alk. paper)
        1. United States—Popular culture—History—20th century.
    2. United States—Social life and customs—1918-1945.   I. Title.
E169.1.B4926   1993
973.9—dc20   93-2855

TP

British Library Cataloguing in Publication Data is available.

Library of Congress Catalog Card Number: 93-2855
ISBN: 0-275-94395-X

First published in 1993

Praeger Publishers, 88 Post Road West, Westport, CT 06881
An imprint of Greenwood Publishing Group, Inc.

Printed in the United States of America

(∞)™

The paper used in this book complies with the
Permanent Paper Standard issued by the National
Information Standards Organization (Z39.48-1984).

10 9 8 7 6 5 4 3 2 1

For my wife,
Kapikookalani Best

Contents

Introduction

The picture of the depression years that most of us have is one of unremitting bleakness: of street-corner apple sellers, soup lines, foreclosures, closed factories, armies of unemployed, hunger if not starvation, and labor violence. The contrasts drawn with the decade of the 1920s that preceded it have been stark: a decade of "Fords, Flappers and Fanatics," as George Mowry described it, followed by a decade of "Hard Times," to use the title of Studs Terkel's oral history. The frivolity, fads, and mad speculation of the 1920s came crashing down with the stock market as the decade ended, to be replaced by a decade of down-at-the-heels, worn-at-the-elbow, emphasis on survival—or at least so we assume. Thus, the popular culture of the 1930s has attracted little of the attention directed by historians toward the "roaring twenties."

The 1930s was a decade that defies such easy labeling as has been applied to the 1920s. That decade, we are told, was the "roaring twenties," or the "jazz age," or the "flapper era," or a dozen other easy characterizations. The 1920s unfolds between 1920 and the stock market crash of 1929 without any major demarcations or turning points. The 1930s was not so simple. The depression had scarcely begun when the 1920s ended, but it was a fact of life from the beginning of the 1930s to the end of the decade. That alone meant that much about the 1930s would be dramatically different from the previous decade, and not only in an economic sense. The defeat of Hoover in November 1932 and the inauguration of Roosevelt in March 1933 brought alterations in American life far greater than most people expected from a change of leadership and party in the White House. The inauguration of almost any other leading Democrat as president on that day in March would have brought only mild changes at most. The inauguration of Roosevelt, on the other hand, brought momentous transformations that are with us yet over a half century later.

The apparent upturn in the economy in the mid-1930s, followed by the collapse in 1937 and 1938, marks yet another demarcation. Americans who had good reason to feel that they were riding in a "down" elevator from 1930 to early 1933 found that they had replaced the elevator ride for a roller coaster under Roosevelt. Meanwhile, the tide of events in the rest of the world was also exerting its influence on American life, particularly toward the end of the decade.

Through all of these "micro-eras" of the 1930s, however, there was at least one consistency—unemployment. With between 14.3 percent (1937) and 25.2 percent (1933) of the work force unemployed during the 1930s, many others employed for shorter hours due to an absence of work or because of work-sharing, and still others insecure about the future of their own jobs, the reality or specter of unemployment was obviously an important influence on American behavior during the decade. The growing popularity of psychology since the 1920s, combined with the traumatic conditions of the 1930s, meant that one product of the decade would be the study of the psychology of unemployment.

It is unfortunate that the study of the psychological effects of unemployment was in its infancy at precisely the time in history when its insights might have been most useful. Although the field has become more sophisticated in recent decades, later studies are of only marginal utility in understanding the 1930s. This is true because of a number of differences between the 1930s and more recent decades. No economic recessions of recent times compare with the devastating effects of the Great Depression, which called into question the very viability and survival of the free enterprise system. No economic recessions of recent times brought workers and their families face to face with a sense of shame at their idleness and dependence on charity as did the Great Depression. The precedent of the 1930s has, in fact, served to ameliorate for later generations much that was extremely traumatic for workers and their families during the Great Depression.

In 1938 P. Eisenberg and Paul Lazarsfeld summarized the conclusions that could be drawn from over 100 studies of the unemployed done during the 1930s. In general they found that the unemployed tended to be more unstable emotionally, to have lower morale, and to pass through psychological stages in response to unemployment. In these stages they progressed from initial optimism, through pessimism, to fatalism or resignation as their unemployed situation dragged on over time. As they described it:

We find that all writers who have described the course of unemployment seem to agree on the following points: first there is shock, which is followed by an active hunt for a job, during which the individual is still optimistic and unresigned; he still maintains an unbroken attitude.

Second, when all efforts fail, the individual becomes pessimistic, anxious and suffers active distress: this is the most crucial state of all. And third, the individual becomes fatalistic and adapts himself to his new state but with a narrower scope. He now has a broken attitude.[1]

To put it another way, during the early stages the individual's personality shapes the response to unemployment, but by the latter stages the effect is in the other direction: the fact of unemployment is shaping the individual's personality.

Studies of the unemployed in the 1930s indicated that they significantly reduced their social contacts outside the family, but the early studies paid little attention to other changes in their leisure time pursuits. More recent studies have explored quantitative changes, but not qualitative ones. One study, for example, showed that its unemployed subjects spent more time preparing meals than when they were employed, listened to more radio and watched more television, spent more time window shopping and reading and gardening and doing home repairs, and less time on entertainment that required the expenditure of money.[2] These are results that are not likely to surprise anyone. A more useful pursuit would be to learn if the unemployed were involved in new and perhaps socially less-desirable pastimes in their new condition. Did their tastes in reading, television, and movies change under the impact of unemployment? Are they more prone to illegal, immoral, and unethical activities than when employed? Are their leisure time activities consistent with what we might expect of individuals suffering blows to their egos?

Those studies and others done more recently indicate that the unemployed feel stigmatized by their condition, and that as a consequence they often continue for some time to act as if the condition did not exist. They may, for example, delay as long as possible applying for assistance for themselves and their families, since this would denote acceptance of their condition and expose it to others; they may go on vacation as if this were a normal break in their employment routine rather than the cessation of it; and they may continue as long as possible to spend money at the same level as when they were employed.[3]

Eventually, however, they are forced by circumstances to accept their new condition, and with that acceptance comes a sense of diminished control over the unemployed's own life and those of others. The breadwinning male, for example, whose control over his wife and children has been based on their respect for his earning abilities and dependence upon him for the necessities of life, now finds his status eroded not only in the eyes of his family but in his own, as well.[4] The unemployed tend to feel dehumanized, insignficant. Such a situation can easily lead to feelings of alienation or of depression in the individual's response to unemployment. Typical results are increases in mental hospital admissions, alcoholism, drug abuse, marital violence, family abuse, and the suicide rate.[5]

Moreover, those who suffer from prolonged unemployment are almost always forced into a condition of dependency—on public or private charity, or on the assistance of family members. While such a situation is more accepted today, it was more traumatic during the 1930s when it lacked the precedents that have existed since then. When employed, these people had regarded out-of-work recipients of charity with contempt and disgust, never imagining that they could fall into such a situation. Now, that contempt and disgust was turned on them, not only by the employed but even in their own eyes. The unemployed regarded themselves as inferior, even as they were so regarded by many others.

Two basic psychological needs that we all share are a need for self-esteem and a need for social status. Obviously an important ingredient in attaining both is success, which increases both the values we attach to ourselves and which others attach to us. The unemployed were, by their own definition and that of others, failures rather than successes, and therefore were unable to fulfill either of these needs in what were for them the normal ways. Moreover, they suffered from the insecurity of their position—the lack of definiteness as to what opportunities, emergencies, and responsibilities the next hour or day or week might bring, even how people would react to them in the next social situation.

Such attacks on the ego are, Freud found, countered by essentially four defense mechanisms: repression, projection, reaction formation, and regression. In influencing the popular culture of the 1930s, two of these in particular appear to have been important: repression and regression. Through repression, the individual is able to purge painful realities from conscious awareness, thereby evading feelings of guilt, anxiety, and other psychic conflicts. Regression, on the other hand, finds the individual escaping from stress by reverting to fantasy—usually to an earlier childhood stage of development, in which the behavior exhibited is that which one would expect of a child or adolescent rather than an adult. Modern psychiatry has added many variations of, or additions to, Freud's four basic ego defenses, a number of which are helpful in understanding the behavior of the 1930s. Identification, for example, is useful in understanding the fascination of young women with movie stars during the decade, and Roosevelt's early popularity. Comprehensive studies of ego defenses, in fact, read like a catalog of the popular culture of the 1930s.[6]

Much of the popular culture of the 1930s was clearly attractive for the means it offered to escape from the guilt, anxieties, stresses, and insecurities of the depression years. It was of value, in short, not so much because it filled in idle time as for its repressive role in permitting the individual the opportunity to escape, at least for a time, from the conscious awareness of unpleasant realities. Some aspects of popular culture during the decade were clearly regressive, as in the case of adult participation in children's games and pastimes. Others found Americans identifying with "stars" of one type or another, or with groups.

The preoccupation with one form or another of gambling during the 1930s was revealing of at least two forms of ego defense. As one psychologist put it nearly a century ago, gambling was a "diversion (that which turns aside, distracts), a way of pretending to work, or filling up the blanks in existence, of 'killing time.' "[7] For other psychologists, gambling offered a form of hope for those whose lives seemed otherwise so hopeless.[8] It provided a feeling of expectation, in which, one observed, the future prospect becomes more important than the present reality.[9] At the same time, as another psychologist has observed, gamblers possess a "fanatical belief in infantile megalomania." Like children, they expect that they will win simply because they *want* to win. "Mentally, [the gambler] has regressed to the earlier period in which he was, to all intents and purposes, omnipotent, that is, to infancy, when all his desires were automatically fulfilled."[10]

Much of the popular culture of the 1930s, then, seems to present itself as a study of the effects of unemployment and related economic trauma on leisure time pursuits. This study, however, is intended to be descriptive of that popular culture rather than analytical in the chapters that follow. This brief consideration of psychological influences on the 1930s ought, nevertheless, to demonstrate the complexity of the decade and the difficulties of applying to the popular culture the kinds of simplistic descriptions and explanations so commonly applied to the decade that preceded it. There was much about the popular culture of the 1930s that was ugly and depressing, side by side with as much, or more, that was, and still is, inspiring and beautiful. There was more continuity from the 1920s than one might expect under the circumstances, but other aspects that harkened back even farther in time—to the 1890s. Technological advances influenced American popular culture during the 1930s to a degree unprecedented even in the previous decade, but the poverty of the depression brought back to family life some of the closeness that the technological advances of the first three decades of the century had eroded.

Much of the popular culture of the 1930s seems familiar to us today; some of it, however, is difficult to relate to over a half-century later. The dreariness and desperation of the dance marathons and walkathons—on the part of both the participants and spectators (not to mention the promoters)—seem alien to us today, as if something out of a nightmare. Much of the rest of the popular culture of the decade, however, is reflective to some degree of that same dreariness and desperation if examined closely. Thus, even the fads of the 1930s that duplicated or resembled those of the 1920s were indulged in for very different reasons during the depression than those which had motivated people during the previous decade.

Straitened economic circumstances meant that it was a decade in which the nickel and dime achieved an importance unprecedented then or since, with each of the coins more precious for consumers than in prosperous times. For housewives trying to feed a family of four on $1 per day or less, the cost per-person per-meal was less than a dime.

In another respect the heightened importance of nickels and dimes was the result of a combination of the speculative fever of the 1920s and the depression of the 1930s. The real estate and stock market "plungers" of the 1920s were replaced in the 1930s by millions who gambled on a smaller scale: five-cent chances in a punchboard or jar game, or a ten-cent investment in a chain letter.

And finally, the 1930s would deserve description as the nickel and dime decade if only because of all the devices that appeared during those years to separate Americans from those coins—from dime beer to pinball machines to parking meters, from jukeboxes to comic books. Even technology and entrepreneurship in the 1930s, then, seemed to focus to a considerable degree on the nickels and dimes in the pockets of Americans. Not surprisingly, the director of the U.S. Mint reported that in 1935 nearly three times as many nickels and dimes had been coined as in 1934, because of the many new uses to which they were being put.[11] Simplistic as it is, *The Nickel and Dime Decade* seems as useful as any other title in describing the contents of this book.

As one who was born two months before Roosevelt's first reelection in 1936, I have always been fascinated by the decade. My childhood recollections of the late 1930s and early 1940s include many of the pastimes described in the pages that follow—the jar games and punchboards, curling up in front of the Stromberg-Carlson console to listen to favorite radio programs, and the almost daily appearance at our door by transients seeking food to take back to their packing-crate shantytowns near the railroad tracks. When I read in school later that such shantytowns had been referred to as "Hoovervilles" before March 1933, I wondered what name should be applied to those that still existed after seven years of the Roosevelt presidency.

In the research and writing of this book I have received again the exemplary support that I have begun to take for granted from the director of the University of Hawaii at Hilo Library, Kenneth Herrick, and his fine staff. Dan Eades, history editor at Praeger, was also as supportive as usual. I have been badly spoiled by the encouragement I always receive from these two. The most profound debt of all, however, is always owed to my wife Lani, whose presence in my life is the greatest encouragement of all.

CHAPTER ONE

The Setting

IN PERSPECTIVE

American pop culture in the 1930s is best understood if viewed in the broad perspective of the first four decades of the twentieth century. During the period from 1900 to 1940 the American people went through what can only be described as a series of emotional binges that found them championing causes and embracing fads on a scale and with an intensity that invited exploitation by shrewd entrepreneurs and self-serving political figures.

The origin of America's preoccupation with "successive crazes and popular fads" dates from at least the early years of the republic in the late eighteenth century, but, as Foster Dulles observed, the twentieth century found Americans "taking up with still greater vehemence new fads and fancies, and enjoying a succession of varied diversions with an intensity born of the feverish pace of modern life," producing what he called "a kaleidoscopic scene ever since the close of the Golden Nineties." Fads and crazes came and went, with people embracing each in its turn as they "climbed aboard what came to be called the Great American Band-Wagon."[1]

Fads and crazes went beyond such simple preoccupations as bicycling or crossword puzzles to embrace emotional commitments to political and social causes. What was especially remarkable was the swings of the pendulum that these emotional attachments exhibited, which found Americans feverishly embracing a cause or fad one year and just as fervently rejecting it months or years later. One example was the heady idealism of the Wilson years that found Americans marching off to fight

1

the war to make the world "safe for democracy," and then retreating into cynicism and materialism in the 1920s. Another example was the enthusiastic support for prohibition that was followed shortly thereafter by its emphatic rejection. One newspaper observed in mid-1933: "This is an age of reversals and upturns and overturns. The capacity for astonishment is wearing very thin. We have come to accept revolution almost as a matter of course. But even so, acclimated as we are to the impossible, the swift and sweeping change in public sentiment on prohibition is surprising."[2]

In the 1930s the pendulum swung from the veneration of business and its corporate and financial leaders to a rejection of much that the 1920s had held holy. Curiously enough, few historians have recognized the existence of this remarkable emotional imbalance in the American people and its effect on the politics and popular culture of the 1930s. Contemporaries, however, recognized it. *The Saturday Evening Post* wrote, at the end of the first Hundred Days of the Roosevelt administration:

People swing from cause to cause, from slogan to slogan. A few years ago, the New Era was all the cry; now it is the New Deal. We have booms and landslides not only in stocks, real estate and methods of solving the liquor problem, but in political parties, administrations and personalities. People run from one extreme to another; they go on jamborees of emotion and opinion.[3]

Bruce Bliven, editor of the *New Republic*, concluded that "in its volatility, intensity, violence of thought and action and mercurial changeability," the American temperament was "much more Latin than Nordic."[4]

Will Payne observed in *The Saturday Evening Post* in mid-1933 that the New Deal had repealed the prohibition of alcohol, but had installed a variety of new prohibitions through the National Recovery Administration, the embargo on gold ownership, and other programs. Change, he wrote, had come "in an avalanche," and the people had "accepted prohibition as a standard ingredient in Government-and-people relationship to an extent which must astonish the Anti-Saloon League." Americans, he noted, had "cheerfully accepted sweeping dictations and prohibitions in wartime," then had swept them out. "Yet here we are again reverting to the war-time pattern and going far beyond it. An old-fashioned citizen may wonder where the next wave will take us."[5]

A business journal recalled in 1939 the decade that had almost passed:

The people, or many of them, with the madness of the New Era and the resulting crash still frozen in mind, were suffering pangs of conscience. They felt the need of doing penance. . . . To be sure, there lay behind [the New Deal] a rather cold, calculated program of appealing to this and that element in the population with special favors at the hands of Congress, the President and the Secretary of the Treasury, but no one who lived throughout the mad years from 1933 to, say, 1937 or 1938, can for a moment doubt the authenticity of the emotional wave which seemed to sweep this country from shore to shore.[6]

SCAPEGOATS, VILLAINS, AND HEROES

Although the people targeted businessmen, in general, as the scapegoats for the depression, it was bankers, especially, who were pilloried. Roosevelt's first inaugural speech, in March 1933, was very much in tune with this sentiment when he castigated the "money changers" who had been "driven from the temples," and derided the profit motive. Will Rogers observed late in the same year that "the whole country has come to the conclusion that a banker or financier don't know any more about money than a depositor does. So they are willing to let Mr. Roosevelt try his own ideas with it."[7] Columnist Mark Sullivan told a friend: "There are no gods of business or finance left. All the idols have been toppled over. All the brands have become bad. The symbols have turned out to be not what they formerly stood for."[8]

One result of the animosity toward bankers was a plethora of jokes about their low standing in life in the early 1930s. One example was the story of the dog that accidentally bit a banker, and then had to bite two other people to get the taste out of its mouth. A writer in the *American Mercury* wrote:

The title of banker, formerly regarded as a mark of esteem in the United States, has sunk in public estimation to the point at which it is now almost a term of opprobrium. There seems some danger, in fact, that in forthcoming editions of the dictionary it may be necessary to define the word as a peculiar American colloquialism synonymous with rascal, highbinder, and scalawag, and we may even see the day when to be called a son-of-a-banker will be regarded as justifiable ground for the commission of assault and mayhem.[9]

The Economist, a London news journal, dispatched a correspondent to the United States in 1933. He returned to London after three months spent traveling through the eastern half of the nation and told his readers that "the most interesting and significant feature" he had noted was "the change in the objects of popular hero-worship." The "presiding deities" of the 1920s, the financiers and bankers, had "crumbled to the dust in the vast majority of American minds. To be a banker in the United States today is about as unpleasant as it is to be a Jew in Germany or an Outcaste in India." He related a popular joke going around the United States:

"Have you found a job, Dwight old Man?" "Yes, I have, Wilbur old man. I have become the president of a bank. But please, please don't tell my poor old mother. It would break her heart. She still supposes that I am playing the piano in a [whore] house."

It was this attitude, he found, that accounted for much of the people's support of Roosevelt's policies, their position being: "The President's policy doesn't please Wall Street. . . . So now we know for certain that this is the policy for us." The opposition of the bankers and other businessmen to Roosevelt's policies had, in fact, only served "to strengthen the President's position enormously throughout the country," because "the American people have fixed upon their scapegoat and are thirsting for his blood." Disregarding their own contribution to the fever of speculation that had *preceded* the crash, they had cast the banker in "the role of villain" and their attitude toward financial policy was "largely governed today by vindictiveness which springs from the events of yesterday and the day before." This "spirit of revenge," *The Economist* correspondent wrote, tended "to blind people to future consequences of present acts in a way which, to a foreign observer, seems amazing and alarming."[10]

A New York University economics professor observed after a year of the Roosevelt administration:

Whatever the criticisms which may be leveled against the New Deal, its success as melodrama can scarcely be denied. Act follows act in quick succession, and each contains a new thrill. This is indeed a far cry from the days when America kept cool with Coolidge. The present play has a whole series of villains, and the audience cheers as each in turn is overcome by the hero."[11]

The hero, of course, was President Roosevelt. John Blum has written that there was "in the New Deal an element of the midway on Saturday night, an element of the cocky and the gaudy, a kind of bravado," which led its beneficiaries to not only appreciate its benefits but to also revel "in its showmanship."[12]

Popular culture in the 1930s was inevitably influenced by the climate of class antagonism fomented by the Roosevelt administration beginning with the first inaugural speech. *Nation's Business* observed in mid-1934 that the great French statesman Talleyrand had once remarked that the "success of a political party depended upon its ability to make the mass of the people hate somebody or something." Under Roosevelt, it observed,

people were taught to hate Hoover. Now they are taught to hate all the forces which enter into our national business activity. First it was the banks and bankers; then those handling investments; then mortgage holders; then those who furnish power and light; then manufacturers who were chiselers, sweatshop operators, child labor exploiters, rebaters, overproducers. Nor were the oil, coal and timber "barons" overlooked. Then commercial aviation. . . . Just now the communication companies are under fire, and the market places of commodities and stocks and bonds.[13]

Never before had the nation witnessed "such a general and continuous muckraking of our business," the effect of which was to weaken "the faith and confidence of the people in the very institutions they must use to bring back prosperous times."[14]

"Bankers," Professor James L. McCamy observed in 1939, "were prominent among the scapegoats of the recovery era. Symbols like 'money changers,' 'intrenched greed,' 'economic royalists,' or 'the forgotten man' became common in the addresses of the President and other federal officials." The purpose, he wrote, was to shift the people's "loyalty from private to public authority and decision," and thereby make them receptive to the New Deal policies.[15]

SHIFTING VALUES

"Orthodox" economics was discredited. Economists could now be found influencing policy who indicted the profits and savings that resulted from hard work as, in fact, the inevitable causes of depressions such as the one in which the nation was mired. Almost everything that Americans had been taught from infancy to believe in and treasure was suddenly in discard or at least disrepute. White had become black, and black was now white. The federal government, which might have been an anchor against such doubts, had instead become a principal cause. Relating these shifting standards and values to the emotional swings of Americans in the first decades of the twentieth century, *The Saturday Evening Post* wrote: "Surely those who regard the experience of the past, or even the conduct of affairs in the past, as wholly wasted or misdirected are suffering from one of these familiar emotional landslides."[16]

The early legislation of the New Deal came rapidly and was bewildering for most Americans. What did devaluation of the dollar, for example, mean for the average American? Probably many wondered with Westbrook Pegler:

If I am broke at this time and the dollar is reduced by half, does that mean that I am 50 per cent less broke than I was, because the dollar is that much easier to get, or 50 per cent broker because when I do get it, it will take $1.50 to buy what I could now buy for one buck if I had the buck?[17]

With prohibition eliminated and the possession of gold made illegal, one observer pointed out: "It's a changing world. Two years ago if I had $100 in gold in my pocket and you had a bottle of whiskey, you could have been arrested. Now, I could be."[18]

In the midst of poverty and hunger, Americans watched as the New Deal slaughtered pigs that might have become pork and plowed up fields that might have provided food. A woman on welfare wrote in *Scribner's*:

Thrift, industry, self-reliance, fortitude—these virtues have become vices and will destroy the individual who practises them. This is an unpleasant thought, but millions of us today are being forced to accept it. The farmer whose bumper crop is a sin, all those whose savings became hoardings—any one exposed to the economic conditions of today, if his character has been set in the old culture, will find himself hampered by ideas and attitudes which are no longer appropriate. At first this is only bewildering. But as the pressure increases, as adaptation to the new conditions becomes necessary, the bewilderment gives place to pain.[19]

The New Deal, George Sokolsky warned in 1936, was instilling in Americans contempt for hard work, thrift, and the law to a degree that its affect on Americans as human beings could no longer be ignored. "We can survive without potatoes," Sokolsky wrote, "but what are we to be without character?"[20] For obvious reasons, some concluded that the New Deal had created a Lewis Carroll type of America, in which daily scenes seemed to have come from Alice in Wonderland.[21]

THE ASSAULT ON CAPITALISM

In the 1930s a parade of English socialists contributed to this bewilderment and pain when they traveled to the United States and lectured Americans on the evils of the capitalist system, which they were certain was responsible for the world's predicament. Such attacks were difficult to ignore when they came from such household names as George Bernard Shaw and H. G. Wells. Shaw was first, traveling to the United States scarcely a month after Roosevelt's first inauguration. The outspoken Shaw condemned capitalism as "criminal heresy" and "the poison-flower of present-day civilization." He preferred, he said, the rule of a Stalin or a Mussolini to rule by financiers, who were "the destroyers of the State." Wealth, Shaw charged, corrupted a nation, and Americans must take control of America away from "the bankers and great industrialists."[22]

Such statements as Shaw's only gave greater respectability to the assault already launched by the Roosevelt administration against bankers and businessmen. Traditional American liberalism—or progressivism, to use the term current before the 1930s—had sought to curb business malpractices, but had not been directed against the free enterprise system or against *all* businessmen and bankers as a class. The new Rooseveltian brand of liberalism, however, *was* antibusiness and antibanking, set class against class, and yet articulated no coherent alternative to the free enterprise economy it set out systematically to sabotage.[23]

Liberal journals quickly adopted the new antibusiness liberalism, much to the discomfiture of veteran progressives/liberals like Amos Pinchot and, later, Walter Lippmann. Pinchot scolded the editors of *The Nation* for going "clean away from liberalism into communism." He was convinced, he wrote, that liberalism had "far more power to do something useful and fundamental in this country than has the communist philosophy."[24] Pinchot suggested to the editor of a new liberal magazine that it follow the line of "a magazine frankly defending capitalism, with all its drawbacks, as the best economic system devised so far, but pointing out that the privileges which are undermining, and in fact destroying, capitalism, must be prevented by the operation of law, and also I think by the force of public opinion." Such a position would, Pinchot thought, appeal "to lots of people who are sick of the communist drivel, and who don't believe in socialism or think that it's practicable in the U.S.A."[25] The problem with those around Roosevelt, he wrote a friend, was that they were essentially settlement workers rather than economists, who knew nothing about American business and its needs. "After all, we are a business, industrial and farming country. And we've got to encourage production if we are to encourage reemployment."[26] Capitalism, for all of its faults, was "the only system which has brought any degree of freedom to people anywhere in the world."[27]

Because of his commitment to capitalism, Pinchot broke with the new breed of liberals when asked to join organizations or sign statements that he regarded as anticapitalist. He told the National Unemployment League that he could not sign a statement of theirs because "the drafters of the petition do not really believe in private industry or in the profit system, and, therefore, they are in another pew from me."[28] Pinchot also resigned as chairman of the People's League for Economic Security when it went "too far to the left."[29] It was embarrassing, Pinchot wrote, for genuine liberals "to have to fight on the same side with economic royalists."[30] But Roosevelt's was "a sort of bogus liberalism, which prevents a realistic liberal movement, and yet accomplishes none of the ends which intelligent people are interested in." The principal objective of that bogus liberalism seemed to be to convince the country "that we must have a brand-new deal with collectivism as the goal."[31]

Harold Stearns examined the effect on American thought of the twin viruses—Marxism and Fascism—that had invaded America with particular impact as a result of the depression. It was, he wrote, a case of a "new and exciting germ of infantilism and obscurantism falling on [an] American intellectual soil" that was "soon to be made fertile with bitterness by the widespread economic collapse." Once in the United States, these viruses had given "a new lease of life" to the tradition of violence and intolerance that had always existed in America. Violence and intolerance now became "intellectually" respectable when it was "ideologically" correct (as in the sit-down strikes of 1937). The approved ideological end, in short, made any means intellectually acceptable. Both doctrines sanctioned force over persuasion, both were contemptuous of democracy, and both were essentially antiintellectual. Considering it from a standpoint that rested on some sense of history, one could not avoid, Stearns wrote, the impression of being "in a kind of psychiatric Alice-in-Wonderland."[32]

A prominent Catholic—editor-in-chief of both *America* and *Thought*—found American democracy in the late 1930s in more danger than at any time during the nineteenth century. The Roosevelt administration had "introduced new concepts of social and governmental relations that are influencing American civilization"; "the ideologies of Communism, Fascism, Nazism are leaping the ocean and spreading in the United States." The "so-called American Liberals, who have always been as sentimental as they are mutable, are being infected with un-American ideas, and the American proletariat is being mobilized for social redress." But in opposing these trends, he wrote, "American Catholics are not supported . . . by official Protestantism and Judaism." On the contrary, their religious leaders were "so hysterically combating Fascism and Nazism that they are being encircled by Communism."[33]

The virus of class antagonism and conflict that was exploited and given respectability by the Roosevelt administration naturally infected American culture in the 1930s—especially literature, drama, and scholarly writing. As Robert Spiller observed, those American writers who were not expatriates "were attracted by the extremist movements of Communism and Fascism at home. Acceptance of the doctrine of Marx in its most dogmatic form became the badge of the 'radical' critic of 1930–1940." Magazines were taken over by extremists, and "writers of fiction, poetry, and drama, as well as of criticism, became critics of the democratic tradition and the capitalist order rather than, like the earlier Literary Radicals, advocates at most of reform."[34] In short, many in the literary arts were making the same transition that was occurring in American political "liberalism." What Joseph Wood Krutch observed of playwrights was true also of many authors and Hollywood scriptwriters: namely, that they began in the early 1930s to view their works as "weapons" against the capitalist establishment and to express "a point of view near that of the communist if not avowedly identical with it."[35]

One result of this was that few read the proletarian writers of the 1930s. These writers abandoned the fashionable contempt for the masses of the 1920s, popularized by H. L. Mencken and others, and sought to portray the lives and issues of what Dixon Wecter called "the 'little people'—the down-and-outers, waifs and strays always present, whom the jazz age loftily had ignored." Some, but not all of them, were motivated by Marxist or near-Marxist views of class struggle and conflict. The best and most enduring of the variety were James T. Farrell's Studs Lonigan trilogy, and the works of John Steinbeck, John Dos Passos, and Thomas Wolfe. The more doctrinaire among the Marxists were inevitably the poorest writers, "as if," Wecter wrote, "Marx's own ineptitude were inherited by his cult."[36]

The impact on the public and on popular culture of this "cultural revolution" in the 1930s was minimal, therefore, since its audience was limited largely to fellow writers and critics who were similarly alienated. Years of economic distress had made many Americans willing to accept "revolutionary," "collectivist," even "dictatorial" government in Washington as long as it came about through familiar institutions and produced economic recovery, but when they went to the movies, opened their magazines, or turned on their radios they wanted escape, not issues.

THE PUBLIC RESPONSE

The American people had rejected Marxist solutions to their plight in the 1932 presidential election, by giving the Socialist, Communist, and Socialist Labor parties a combined total of only about 1 million votes (compared to Roosevelt's 22.8 million and Hoover's 15.7 million), but they now seemed willing to accept the New Deal variety of collectivism if it produced benefits. Those, however, the New Deal did not deliver. Unemployment remained high, and visible symptoms of recovery seemed to have no effect on the number of people requiring relief or on the amount required annually for their sustenance (see table).

Nevertheless, few Americans embraced the class consciousness that was being fomented by the Roosevelt administration and by many intellectuals, writers, and artists. A study of 59 fairly typical unemployed families during the winter of 1935–36 found no such class feeling. The normal situation

Unemployment, 1929–40

Year	Unemployment Rate	Number Unemployed (in millions)
1929	3.2	1,550
1930	8.9	4,340
1931	16.3	8,020
1932	24.1	12,060
1933	25.2	12,830
1934	22.0	11,340
1935	20.3	10,610
1936	17.0	9,030
1937	14.3	7,700
1938	19.1	10,390
1939	17.2	9,480
1940	14.6	8,120

Source: U.S. Department of Commerce, Bureau of the Census, *Historical Statistics of the United States* (Washington, DC, 1975), Vol. I, p. 135.

of the families was somewhere between working class and lower middle class, although all were now on some form of relief. Although invariably "discouraged and despondent over their economic difficulties," the study found that "these men did not become the class-conscious radicals some expected them to become."[37] Most of the men belonged to unions, but they had "little class consciousness. The union was an employment agency, an instrument for improving working conditions without any emotional alignment or identification with the members."[38]

The unemployed breadwinners showed little interest in politics. Many blamed themselves for their difficulties. Others sought scapegoats, including FDR, foreigners, blacks, and the employment of married women in jobs that might be done by unemployed heads of households. Many were critical of the relief system on which they were dependent, including the high salaries that were being paid to administrators, and the failure of relief agencies to hire the unemployed to staff their positions.[39] While some felt that the depression had revealed defects in capitalism that needed to be corrected, they nevertheless wanted the system retained largely intact. Some thought that economic recovery could only come about through a return to Republican policies. The New Deal, one said, had turned out to be a "raw deal." Another man, who had denounced capitalism to the interviewer, nevertheless announced that he would vote Republican in the next election so that the wealthy would be confident enough to invest and get the economy going again.[40]

Another study, of 100 Chicago families in 1934–35, came to similar conclusions. The general attitude of the families, the study found, was "one of docile acceptance" toward the depression. "There is little evidence that these people as a group had been sufficiently interested or aroused by the depression to seek either explanation or any plan of action," the authors of the study wrote. "Few of them had any consciousness of the depression as a class phenomenon affecting in particular certain social classes. It was an individual experience, attributable to unluckiness, to God, or in some vague way to machinery or the rich." As for their attitude toward relief, responses varied from acceptance, resistance to accepting it except as a temporary measure, and resentment toward the relief agencies and case workers.[41] The attitude of most of the Chicago families toward FDR and the New Deal was a positive one, but for very limited reasons. As the authors wrote:

Their approval did not grow out of any hope that the New Deal would reorganize the economic system and perhaps prevent future depressions. They took a much more personal view: the federal government had not let them starve, and it had provided work for the men and C.C.C. camps for the boys. . . . The same apathy regarding an explanation of the depression characterized the attitude toward what might be done to remedy this depression and prevent future depressions. With but few exceptions people were concerned only in so far as the depression touched them personally.[42]

Given Roosevelt's vaunted popularity among the "masses," it is interest-ng that these two studies, both of them made well into the New Deal years and before the 1936 presidential election, show so little enthusiasm for either Roosevelt or the New Deal, except as dispensers of the federal alms that many of the respondents were dependent upon. Among those few who voiced an opinion on the prospects of recovery, there was a conviction that Roosevelt and the New Deal were not the answer. From such studies, combined with the Gallup Polls of 1936 (as well as the Democrats' own poll), it seems clear that Roosevelt's lopsided victory over Landon in 1936 did not result from approval of the New Deal reforms or from Roosevelt's popularity, but rather from federal relief expenditures. Those suffering most from the depression might realize that a change of administration was desirable in order to produce recovery *from* the depression (as indicated in the early polls), but as election day approached they were forced to confront a grim reality: that despite their opposition to Roosevelt and their criticism of the relief system, there was no other apparent source of relief money *during* the depression than the Roosevelt administration's relief agencies.

In her travels among the youth of the country, Maxine Davis found little evidence of radicalism even on college campuses that were regarded as heavily infected with it. At one such school, the University of Chicago, she found that the Student League for Industrial Democracy contained only 45–50 members, while the Communist group had about 25. Their classmates, she learned, regarded them as "either maladjusted and neurotic" or unable to find any other place to go.[43] The University of North Carolina, likewise tarred for its "radicalism," was found to contain "six staunch followers of Stalin," and the University of California numbered about 35 members in the local communist campus organization out of a study body of about 12,500. At Columbia University, students and faculty estimated that between 5 and 10 percent of the students were at the far left, with an equal number at the far right.[44] "Radicalism" on the campuses, Davis found, was characterized more by a "gimme" attitude than by a zeal for reform or revolution.

Similarly, few were interested in politics in general, but many of those who were seemed to have more interest in patronage than in princi-ples.[45] Davis found that the "zeal for change brought in by the Roosevelt Administration" had already flickered into indifference, and pity for the underprivileged had given way "to mounting irritation at the cost of maintaining them." As a high school senior in Cleveland put it, most of them were not enthuastic about the New Deal, few even knew what it was all about. They were aware that Roosevelt was "giving away" money to the "so-called needy." They felt that even though their "parents are paying for it, . . . what good is it doing us?" There was still, Davis found, a sentimental attachment to Roosevelt on the part of young and parents alike for his efforts to help them, but they were cynical of his ability to do so.[46]

Youth, Davis wrote, was searching for a hero—someone to admire, to imitate, to follow—but there was none who inspired the 1930s generation as so many had in the 1920s. The athletes of the 1930s did not attract the devotion of a Babe Ruth or a Jack Dempsey in the 1920s, nor were the movie stars of the 1930s the equals of Mary Pickford or Rudolph Valentino. Captains of industry had fallen from their lofty perches, and politicians had not replaced them. Even the demagogues of the Huey Long variety attracted little attention among youth.[47]

Most young people, Davis was surprised to find, exhibited an "uncom-plaining acceptance" of the consequences of the depression for them: unemployment (or underemployment), delayed marriage, and all the rest. Many were cynical about Roosevelt and the New Deal, one observing that Roosevelt had done nothing for his father and nothing for him, other than to provide "three squares and a bed" in the New Deal "transient dumps." He would, he told Davis, be a "goddam fool" to work when he could give a false name and loaf in the transient camps. "You go home and tell Roosevelt that every time the gravy train starts this baby's gonna be on it," he told her.[48]

Reflecting the lack of real improvement for most people is the fact that the number of suicides remained fairly constant between the Hoover and Roosevelt years, despite the greater attention given to them in the former by historians. However, deaths by "accidental falls" increased markedly under the New Deal to the highest rate ever, suggesting that some of the falls were not accidental at all. A single issue of the New York *Herald-Tribune* (for October 22, 1935) reported the following presumed suicides after two-and-half-years of the New Deal, some of which might have been classified by the authorities as "accidental falls"; a 69-year-old Philadelphia insurance broker who "leaped or fell" from the 16th floor of a New York City hotel; a 59-year-old executive of a wholesale textile firm who shot himself with a .32 calibre revolver due to "financial reverses"; a 51-year-old lady who jumped or fell from the roof of an apartment house; a 60-year-old unemployed (since July) man who jumped from a 14th floor window after he failed to get a job; a 31-year-old baker who gassed himself; and a 54-year-old owner of a shoe-repair shop who hanged himself.

To such stories could be added others to illustrate how desperate the lot of many Americans continued to be after years of Roosevelt and the New Deal. A single issue of the Washington *Post* (of December 8, 1935) contained the following two heart-rending stories: (1) In Baltimore a 23-year-old man hanged himself in his jail cell only hours after police had arrested him for tapping a gas main for heat after the electricity and gas had been turned off for nonpayment; he left behind a 19-year-old wife and a 3-year-old child, a younger child having died in January of double pneumonia. His relief checks had been too intermittent to support his family. His wife found him hanging in his cell with a picture of his child in his hand. (2) An unemployed New York City man went to Schenectady to look for work. He was successful, and wrote his wife and daughter in New York to join him. The letter went to the wrong address. In the meantime, his despairing wife had turned on the gas in their flat, killing herself and the daughter.

These incidents, just a few of multitudes that can be found in the newspapers of the Roosevelt years, occurred when Roosevelt was telling the American people "We are on our way!" The shattering downturn that occurred in 1937 and 1938 dispelled that hope even farther, turned the people away from the antibusiness biases they had shared with the New Deal, and produced a resurgence of Republican political strength.

But who were Democrats and who were Republicans in the 1930s? There was good reason to be confused. Roosevelt and the new Deal abandoned the Democratic Party's traditional Jeffersonian distrust of a strong federal government and commitment to states' rights, while the Republican Party, in opposition to the New Deal trend toward an all-powerful federal government, began to sound more and more like the pre-1933 Democrats than their Hamiltonian traditions. The Des Moines *Register* found the two parties "almost bumping into each other since 1932 in their haste to trade sides on the issue of states' rights." It was "one of the most astonishing developments in modern American politics." It was also "one of the most embarrassing and confusing developments to the case-hardened members of both parties." Both parties, it found, were embarrassed by the views of their founders, and it wondered: "If Jefferson and Hamilton were to return to the vastly extended scene of their labors, which party would which venerated father claim as his own baby now?"[49] Alice Roosevelt Longworth, daughter of Teddy Roosevelt, agreed that there had been "a tendency for one side to edge in on the other side's [patron] saint," with the Democrats quoting Lincoln and the Republicans quoting Jefferson. "The next step," she wrote, "if the Democrats are consistent, will be to install Alexander Hamilton among their seraphim."[50] The American people had many reasons to be confused during the 1930s.

Many Americans had more time to devote to popular culture in the 1930s, including quite a number who continued to be employed. One business response to the depression was to reduce hours of employment, partly to cut expenses and partly to reduce layoffs, by spreading the lessened amount of available work among as many workers as possible. Businesses that had not voluntarily reduced the workweek by 1933 found that it was now a requirement under the National Recovery Administration (NRA) codes, and even after the NRA was found unconstitutional by the Supreme Court, most businesses continued the practice of the five-day workweek and the two-day work-free weekend. In 1937 the National Industrial Conference Board reported: "While five years ago the five-day week was exceptional, it has now become quite general."[51] In short, both employed and unemployed Americans found themselves with additional days of leisure at a time when they could least afford to fully enjoy them. The combination of the two factors affected every aspect of popular culture during the 1930s, from fads to spectator sports.

The popular culture of the 1930s was also affected by the high drama of New Deal experiments like the National Recovery Administration, the charisma of the omnipresent Roosevelt, and the administration's rhetoric devoted to the least fortunate one-third of the population.

CRIME

In one study of the 1930s, Charles Hearn found that

in some works of the thirties, including a good many popular-magazine stories, one detects what is essentially a "cult of failure" in which all the virtue and dignity of the world are portrayed as residing in the failures and losers while all the viciousness and cruel exploitation are the province of the "successes."

The businessmen "heroes" of popular magazine fiction in the 1920s were now replaced by professionals and working-class people, and biographical articles shifted from businessmen as subjects to celebrities in government, sports, and other fields. Moreover, many writers found commercial success in encouraging the kind of shift in American values that Roosevelt had called for beginning with his first inaugural speech.[52]

Such a climate of shifting values, standards, and morals, in which what had been good was often bad, and vice versa, encouraged criminal (antisocial) behavior and a reevaluation of criminals. Crime flourished in the 1930s, both as a way of life and as a preoccupation of popular culture. It was a violent decade, with arrests in America more than doubling between 1932 and 1939. Newspapers and orators inveighed against the "crime wave" that was sweeping across the country, and the front pages of the more sensation-seeking journals featured stories of the latest criminal adventures: from the slaying of John Dillinger, at last, outside a Chicago movie theater, to the exploits of "Pretty Boy" Floyd and "Baby Face" Nelson.

As if reality were not enough, moviemakers, writers, and radio dramatists made criminals and the fight against crime prominent subjects of popular culture during the decade. The early 1930s, especially, Hearn says, saw the glorification of the "gangster-tough guy," who represented "yet another response to the failure of the American dream in a crisis period: that is, a hard-boiled, tough, violent, antisocial, lawless response." He represented, Hearn concluded, "a perversion of the conventional myth of success, and yet in his career the raw ingredients of the rags-to-riches success story could be observed."[53]

One of the most interesting crimes of the 1930s was one that combined the corporate success story of the 1920s and the rags-to-riches gangster theme of the 1930s. The New York *Times* said of the Philip Musica case: "Not in the days of the 'Arabian Nights,' of Jules Verne, of Daniel Defoe or any of our modern mystery writers has there been any imagined figure whose career matches that of this man." Musica, an exconvict, had "laid aside the fugitive, caught, sentenced, disgraced," and had "manufactured the very model of an important, respected business man." Using the name Frank Donald Coster, Musica rose to the top of one of the most respected pharmaceutical companies in America, McKesson & Robbins, surrounded himself with relatives and cronies, and proceeded to bilk the company of millions of dollars. Before he was caught and unmasked, Musica was living the life that most Americans dreamed of while sitting in their movie theater seats—a life of country clubs, country homes, and yachts.[54]

POPULAR CULTURE

Despite the depression, the 1930s was a decade of great technological advances, many of which affected popular culture. Citing developments in the radio, movie, and publishing industries, Alice Marquis wrote: "Never before had technology been so intimately entwined with culture" as it was in the 1930s.[55] Elmer Davis observed early in the decade: "The typical American consumes his leisure by the use, active or passive, of a machine—the automobile, the radio, the motion picture."[56]

And yet the effects of the changes made popular culture in the 1930s seem in a variety of ways closer to the late nineteenth century than to the previous decade of the 1920s. At the beginning of the 1930s, Walter B. Pitkin could still write that one of the most "striking" aspects of American life was "the brief time spent at home," with the average citizen and his children "never home except when they have to be; they seem to feel out of place there. They eat and sleep within its walls, then rush off to work, to school, to the movies."[57] But only a few years later the Lynds' observed that the backyard had become a focus of family life in Middletown, making the life-style resemble that of the 1880s. A better analogy might have been drawn with the 1890s, another decade afflicted with a deep economic depression. The emphasis on home entertainment— whether radio, reading, games, puzzles, gardening, or others—and family "togetherness" resembled the 1890s, and such fads of the 1930s as bicycle riding caused the bike paths and streets of towns and cities to resemble those of 40 years earlier more than those of the previous decade. Clearly a great change in home life occurred during the 1930s under the impact of the depression.

In other ways, however, the 1930s was a clear continuation of the frenzies of the 1920s. John Steinbeck recalled one aspect of the frenzies of the previous decade: "In our little town, bank presidents and track-workers rushed to pay phones to call brokers. Everyone was a broker, more or less. At lunch hour, store clerks and stenographers munched sandwiches while they watched the stock boards and calculated their pyramiding fortunes. Their eyes had the look you see around the roulette table."[58] Many Americans did not lose that "look" in the 1930s. If we can regard the speculation in the stock market as a fad of the 1920s, then certainly we will see a continuation of it in the 1930s, albeit in even sillier forms. America, one observer commented, was "a manic-depressive case." When in the "dumps," Americans sought relief in manic amusements.[59]

In such statements there is a clue to understanding much of the popular culture of the 1930s that in many cases seems so unexplainable. Many of the amusements of that decade have been explained as devices to fill in the idle hours of the unemployed or underemployed. No doubt they filled that need for many. But the popularity of the fads and crazes and other aspects of 1930s popular culture was not limited only to this group, so another explanation must be sought. It is that the popular culture of the 1930s not only filled idle hands, but also distracted worried minds. Americans sought escape from reality not only in radio and movies and pulp magazines, but also in their games. Adults were as likely as children to be found playing games in the 1930s, including the games of their childhood years, like jackstraws. As a writer in the New York *Times* wrote: "It is the grown-ups who have brought about the present game boom. Staid people who want something else to think about gladly become as little children."[60]

Adults were in the grip of forces they could not understand and over which they had no control. Many were forced into the demeaning role of accepting what was still popularly regarded as charity, while many others faced the prospect that they would have to follow suit if conditions did not improve. Their discomfiture can be seen in studies that revealed their contempt for fellow welfare recipients. Demeaned by, but dependent on, welfare, they sought pastimes that dulled or distracted minds that did not want to cope with reality. It is this aspect of the 1930s that gives even the most frivolous pursuits of the decade an underlying sense of desperation.

In sum, the 1930s was a complex decade—more complex than most because of the variety of political and economic and social changes that assaulted Americans in their day-to-day living and that taxed their ability to understand the environment in which they lived. And the popular culture of the decade is all the more interesting for having been a product of such a period. More than most others, a full understanding of the period requires a study of its popular culture.

CHAPTER TWO

Fads and Crazes

THE JIGSAW PUZZLE CRAZE

In many respects the fads and crazes of the 1930s resembled those of the 1920s; others were actually resurrections of even earlier fads. Whether old or new, they showed the subtle influences of the depressed economic conditions of the decade. The fads of the 1930s tended to be cheaper and more time consuming, reflecting a reality of the 1930s: that people had more time than money available. They also tended to be more home-oriented. And, while the fads of the 1930s were, if anything, even daffier and more numerous than those of the 1920s, one can detect in many of them a sense of desperation, a need to escape reality, that was rarely present in those of the the previous decade.

Above all, the 1930s was the decade of games and puzzles—not only for children, but also for adults. The country, said one writer, was "game-minded in the home and elsewhere—on a scale of which no other period had any idea and there are game factories running full-blast with night shifts and assembly belts which they say cannot keep up with orders." It was, he added, "the grown-ups who have brought about the present game boom."[1] Another observer noted that while most of the games sold in stores could be played by both adults and children, at least 30 percent of them—"many more than in the past"—were designed for adults alone.[2] The games and puzzles of the decade, another writer noted, catered to two desires: "(a) something to occupy idle hands, and (b) a chance to win something." Americans of the 1930s, he wrote, had "shown a tendency to take a chance—a chance on almost anything—which not even the frontier days of derring-do and faro could equal in volume."[3]

There was first a brief renewal of the 1920s mah-jongg fad, but just as in the previous decade, mah-jongg was quickly eclipsed by a puzzle. In the 1920s it had been the crossword puzzle, but in the 1930s mah-jongg was supplanted by the jigsaw puzzle, which was in a variety of ways much more representative of the temper and diversions of the 1930s. Picture puzzles were of course nothing new, but earlier versions had been handcut from wood and were expensive. In the spring of 1932 the mass-produced, die-cut jigsaw puzzle was introduced, given away first as premiums to buyers of particular brands of toothpaste, then of mouthwash and milk of magnesia. McKesson and Robbins, Pepsodent, and Listerine each distributed a million, and the demand suggested profit-making possibilities.

By the fall jigsaw puzzles had swept the country like wildfire. Not only were they being sold in stores ranging from 10- and 20-cent versions at Woolworth's to more expensive and elaborate versions at department stores, but they were also being marketed through newstands and neighborhood stores, as well as by hawkers on railroads and subways. Some department stores, like Marshall Field's in Chicago, even began to rent jigsaw puzzles at a modest fee with no deposit required.

Reporting on the phenomenon, one writer observed that "the country, or a large part of it, is on a jig-saw jag." At a time when, due to "stress and strain of depression days, . . . most persons have more time than money and are forced to stay at home nights pursuing low-cost amusements," an estimated 2–2.5 million jigsaw puzzles were being sold weekly in the country, with many others rented out or loaned by buyers to their friends.[4] Clearly a staggering number of Americans were poring over the puzzles any given evening of the week. *Forbes* magazine reported that "in some stores of the Woolworth chain there are times when only those customers with the strongest shoulders or the greatest patience can get to the sales counters."[5] There were "puzzles of the week" and "weekly jigs," jigsaw puzzle clubs, and jigsaw competitions at parties. The pictures tended for the most part to be historical—of the Pilgrims, of colonial landscapes, knights in armor, masterpieces of art, and rural settings—but there were also pictures of movie and radio stars, who allowed their likenesses to be used in exchange for a royalty, and puzzles could even be made from photographs of one's baby or sweetheart or oneself.[6]

In seeking to explore the reasons for their popularity, writers found puzzle addicts reporting that they liked jigsaws because they drove them crazy, or because they could be done without thinking, or that they kept one from worrying. From such responses, one might almost conclude that jigsaw puzzles were a lower-cost and safer method of escape than inebriation. Booze was illegal, although available. However, the genuine article was expensive, the cheaper imitations hazardous to one's health. It is perhaps no mere coincidence that the end of the jigsaw craze occurred at approximately the same time as the legalization of beer.

Psychologists opined that the popularity of puzzles originated in one of mankind's fundamental desires: the need to finish what they set out to do. In a decade when so many problems seemed unsolvable, the jigsaw puzzle offered the opportunity for one to derive the satisfaction of solving at least one small puzzle in a world of larger and more difficult ones. If so, then perhaps it is instructive that the craze died early in 1933 just as the efforts of the Roosevelt administration to solve the greater puzzle of the depression began to captivate the attention of the public, and as those efforts, themselves, began to take on the appearance of pieces in a bewildering puzzle. Others saw in the fad another manifestation of the movement back to "home and hearth," which had characterized family life since the onset of the depression.

At its zenith, during the puzzles' brief heyday between September 1932 and March 1933, Americans purchased an estimated 10 million of them per week, with the three leading manufacturers who specialized in low-priced puzzles for premium and dime store distribution producing between 60 and 70 million alone. With other manufacturers added, the total number of jigsaw puzzles produced during the boom months probably amounted to some 100 million. Producers of paperboard and boxes worked feverishly during those months to meet the demand for jigsaw material and the boxes in which they were packed. The brief flurry of employment in their industries that was provided by the fad, however, soon died with the fad itself.

SKATING AND BICYCLING

By the middle of 1933 the jigsaw craze had passed, to be replaced by a boom in roller skating and a renewed interest in bicycling. Standard four-wheel skates were available for from $1–2 per pair. Children roped off streets to create areas where they could play roller skate polo. The real boom, however, was among older riders, where, *Business Weeks* observed, roller skating and bicycling had "not claimed the attention of many adults in over 30 years."[7] Bicycling clubs began to proliferate by the summer of 1933, and cyclists became common sights on the streets and park paths of every city and town, as they had not been since the 1890s.

Manufacturers were hard-pressed to keep up with the sudden demand for adult-sized bicycles and skates after producing almost exclusively for the juvenile market for years. One manufacturer was forced to crowd a whole year's normal production of skates into three months to supply its regular customers. Another was showing sales of 60–80 percent above 1932. In bicycles the biggest demand was among women, perhaps copying the popularity of bicycles among actresses in Hollywood, with sales of women's bicycles double normal in early 1933. Part of the reason, *Business Week* speculated, was no doubt the prevailing economic conditions that had forced reductions in spending on other forms of amusement.[8] *Forbes* found skate manufacturers agreed that the interest in roller skating, at least, was "a 'depression amusement'—inexpensive, time-consuming and a lot of fun."[9] For those who couldn't afford the price of a bicycle it was often possible to rent one. A University of Michigan graduate student financed his way through school by acquiring and renting 20 bicycles, for which he took such things as fraternity pins, slide rules, watches, and fountain pens for deposits.[10]

THE ENDURANCE MANIA

One unattractive source of fads during the 1930s was the endurance mania of the depression years, even though, like many of the fads of the 1930s, this one, too, had precursors in the 1920s. Comparable to the flagpole sitters of the 1920s, of whom Shipwreck Kelly was the most famous, were the tree-sitters of the 1930s. Youths roosted in trees for days and nights in the hope of capturing a mythical record and gaining publicity for themselves. Some fell from their perches and suffered injuries; at least one was struck by a bolt of lightning. Frederick Lewis Allen told of one boy who was sued by the owner of the tree in which he sat, whereupon his friends cut a branch from another tree and carried him to it so that his vigil would not be interrupted.[11]

Yet the boys were not quite as foolish as some accounts have it. Allen, for example, omits the detail that at the foot of most trees a coin box was prominently displayed, into which onlookers and supporters deposited nickels and dimes. This income, plus a small amount sometimes gained from the sale of autographs, made tree-sitting more profitable than idling away the summer. *Literary Digest* observed that "the bank accounts of the numerous contestants from the sale of autographs, publicity mediums [some wore advertising for local merchants], and outright donations at coin-boxes are not to be dismissed with a shrug." Tree-sitting could, in fact, be so profitable that occasionally mothers and sisters of the boys were also drawn into the trees! In some cities, however, the authorities took a dim view of the hazards of the "sport" and compelled tree-sitters to abandon their perches to the squirrels.[12]

Some blamed the adult generation for setting a bad example for children. "Adult infantilism," as displayed in egg-eating, doughnut-eating, gum-chewing, coffee-drinking, radio-listening, talking, and other kinds of silly "feats" of endurance, were responsible, they concluded, for this aberrant behavior of the young.[13] One "adult," for example, spent 30 days pushing a peanut up Pike's Peak with his nose to win a $500 bet. Others engaged in eating marathons—clams, raw eggs, spaghetti, or whatever else was available. Youngsters embarked on bicycling marathons, then team bicycle marathons, while girls undertook seesaw marathons. It was enough already in 1930 for Nunnally Johnson to proclaim the era as the "Golden Age for Filberts."[14]

Entrepreneurs quickly found ways to combine the bicycling and roller-skating fads with the aforementioned endurance mania to produce new spectator "sports." In bicycling the six-day bicycle race was the result. Fifteen 2-man teams pedaled $100, 19-pound cycles around an O-shaped pine-board track, with team members alternating their stints on the boards. The team member not on the track rested in the infield on a cot in a shelter that looked like a flag-draped crate. The races were punctuated by sprints —races within the race—that were held in series of ten, five times each day. During the racing "season," bicycle racers might participate in a dozen or more six-day races in rapid succession, and it was not unusual for the events to attract crowds of 100,000 over the duration of the spectacle. Racers earned $75 to $500 per day, depending on their value as attractions.[15]

Six-day bicycle races were not a product of the 1930s, having been around since at least the teens and popular in New York City in the 1920s. In the 1930s, though, they assumed the dimensions of a craze and spread to the rest of the country. Originally, a ticket entitled one to endure the entire six days, and as one observer wrote, patrons could remain "just as long as they could stand up under the diet of hot dogs and beer, and a material portion of the spectators arrived when the race started on Sunday and were swept into the alley with the cigar stubs the next Sunday night." The races were also an ideal arena for the light-fingered, with pickpockets relieving the crowd of everything from their wallets to their overcoats. By 1935, however, a ticket bought a patron of the "sport" only one day's attendance at the races, thus fattening the gate receipts.[16]

For roller skating the new "sport" was the Roller Derby, which was roughly modeled after the six-day bicycle races. As devised by its inventor, Leo "Bromo" Seltzer, the Roller Derby was a race of nearly 4,000 miles on roller skates around an oval track in which two-person teams—one male and one female—competed. Unlike the six-day bicycle races, which continued nonstop around the oval track for the duration of the race, Roller Derby contestants raced only from 1:30 p.m. to 12:30 a.m. daily, the two members of the team alternating in 15-minute stints. Like the six-day bicycle races, the team member who was not on the track rested on a cot in the center of the arena while the other circled the track.

A map at the end of the arena showed the progress of the contestants along a zigzag course that stretched from San Diego, California, to New York City in increments of approximately 100 miles between "stopovers" in towns and cities along the route. A Roller Derby typically lasted for about 35 days, with the action occasionally punctuated by "jams," in which the skaters tried to steal laps from one another for additional prize money. These frequently resulted in pile-ups at 35 miles per hour from which the contestants emerged with broken bones that needed resetting and gashes that required stitches from the physicians and nurses who were in attendance for such eventualities. Usually, however, the damaged skater was back on the track before long to relieve the partner who had been required to skate the extra time while repairs were being made.

Crowds at a Chicago Roller Derby in 1936 averaged 10,000 per day. Contestants in that derby included a butcher, a candy wrapper, a steel mill worker, a commercial artist, a French sailor, a golf-club maker, a girl who claimed to be a cousin of former president Herbert Hoover, several husband-and-wife teams, and even a mother-and-son combination.[17] Asked why they submitted themselves to such torture, contestants spoke of the challenge of competing with the best and fastest skaters in the country, since only winners of amateur and professional racing events were allowed to participate. They also spoke of the thrill they received from the cheers of the crowds, and of the companionship they experienced in their little world of skaters. As one of them put it, "When you win a Roller Derby you are beating the best skaters who ever lived."[18] Prizes ranged from $1,000 for a first-place finish to $250 for third, plus the additional awards for "jams" and sprints.

Another aspect of the endurance craze, what one magazine called "dementia Americana," was the dance marathons of the early 1930s. Although quintessentially a depression-era craze, marathon dancing actually originated in 1928, well before the crash. For some unfathomable reason, the morbid interest of large numbers of Americans seemed to be drawn to watching exhausted couples drag each other across dance floors all over the country in marathons that might run continuously for from one to six months. Social workers were especially concerned over the effects the marathons exerted on the physical and moral health of the young girls who followed the marathons from town to town, thereby exposing themselves "to all sorts of physical and emotional excitement and demoralizing influences." The chairman of the Girls' Protective Council wrote:

Couples who win favor are showered with money, called a "spray," often as much as $30 or $40 a night. Many girls receive gifts of clothing, jewelry and even money from marathon fans. The girls frankly say that the two partners take turns sleeping, literally carrying each other while continuing to shuffle along. When a girl becomes a favorite with an audience the management often arranges a solo act for her and her partner, crooning perhaps, or broadcasting her impressions of the marathon— with her feet moving all the time of course.[19]

Yet marathon dancing also brought couples together on a more permanent basis. A writer for *Collier's* found that each marathon always produced wedding bells for some pairs of the dancers. The possibility of matrimony was, in fact, the motive behind some entries. Other participants were "frank enough to confide that if there was nothing else in it, being fed and sheltered for six or seven weeks was an inducement in jobless times."[20]

Marathoners, however, could earn money in a variety of ways. Crowd favorites were frequently showered with coins, even bills, once the field had been thinned to just a few couples. Other marathoners could attract similar "showers" by singing, whistling, or demonstrating some other talent on the dance floor. Terrible singers could attract money from a crowd willing to pay for their silence! Thus, many marathoners found that they could earn $20–$30 per week, in addition to board and eight— yes eight—meals per day.[21]

The dance marathons spawned numerous offshoots, including rock-a-thons (in rocking chairs), talking marathons, roller-skating marathons, and pie-eating marathons. "All," wrote one observer, "are equally silly, all are equally sad; but the dance marathon, more than any other, reveals human nature at its worst." It was, he wrote, "brutality, the sight of others in mental and physical anguish that gives beholders a greedy delight," the "eternal fascination of the kill," which in the case of the marathons was "spiced by sex."[22] Another critic called the marathons "a macabre modern equivalent of a homicidal Roman gladiatorial spectacle."[23] One of the most interesting of the imitators, however, was the kissathons, which also enjoyed a brief vogue, with a Chicago couple holding the record in early 1934 for having "kissed without a break" for six hours and thirty-seven minutes.[24]

Another direct relative of the dance marathon was the walkathon. Seltzer, who devised the Roller Derby, did so after he had first grossed some $2 million promoting walkathons. He staged the first commercial walkathon in Denver, then promoted 22 more before he abandoned them as vulgar, a sentiment that most Americans today would doubtless share. The walkathons were almost identical with dance marathons, except that they lacked even any pretense of dancing. The object was for the two partners to keep moving, or to at least remain upright. Walkathons began with the walkers resting for fifteen minutes out of every hour, but ended with only eight-minute periods of rest and "sprints" of four or five hours without any time off the floor. By this time the survivors had been competing for two months—several thousand hours of continuous walking (shuffling, really)—and the sprints were designed to weed out all but the winners. The contestants circled to the accompaniment of music from an orchestra at one end of the hall and the amplified patter of a succession of masters of ceremony who involved the crowd in rooting on the walkers. These masters of ceremony were, a writer observed, "old minstrel men, medicine men, circus clowns out of a job, racketeers of the old school keeping up with the modern trend."

They play adroitly on the crowd. Their repartee is mostly spontaneous and ranges from clowning to old-fashioned sob stuff. They stand over the fainting couples and lead the applause like band leaders—"Come on folks, give them a hand, show them you're behind them in this hour when they need you. They need you now, folks. Come on—." Then they lead the crowd in a kind of rhythmic ritual of applause which goes, clap—clap—clap—SCREAM—clap—clap—clap—SCREAM.[25]

As contestants dropped out from exhaustion, the masters of ceremony encouraged the audience to reward their efforts by throwing change onto the arena floor. Winners received $1,000.

Critics of the walkathons wondered which were the more pitiful: the pathetic sleepwalkers on the floor, or the mobs of upwards of 10,000 who paid 40 cents (70 cents for ringside seats) admission to feed on their misery. As one wrote:

The mob's excitement, feeding on the tiny bedraggled figures in the arena, is something that at first makes one very sick. Its abandon is awful and shameless. Perhaps this is why ten thousand people go night after night off the streets out of their lonely rooms, to be welded again into a safe mass with their fellows, even it if is only to scream about whether or not Number 34 is going to keep off his knees. . . . Could any nationality except the American sit hour after hour, day after day, watching sick and weary people mill round and round, watching the symbolic dramatization of their own torture of boredom? . . . They recognize the struggle against an unseen, intangible antagonist, a psychological enemy; it has its parallels in their daily life. And the scene gives one a sensation of watching a prolonged calamity, drawn out like an accident, or a moment of crisis that lasts for months. It is startling to realize that the attitudes of the contestants, as they drift wearying over the floor, always keeping on the move, are the attitudes so commonly seen in towns and villages, the normal postures of figures lounging before grocery stores, post offices and poolrooms, a kind of concentration of the American spirit, expressing boredom interrupted by shiftless buffoonery.

The scene was, he wrote, reminiscent of Dante, since the "young bodies aimlessly walking seem so dead, so senseless and so lost." But in the crowds who watched could be seen "the same gestures and the same glazed expressions of fatigue and indifference" as on the faces of the contestants. "Their curious listless wandering is only a shade more animated than that of the walkers in their tortured sleep."[26]

CHAIN LETTERS

Others pursued prosperity almost as pathetically through the mail in the great chain-letter fad of the mid-1930s. The idea apparently began in Denver as a "send a dime" get-rich scheme, but it spread rapidly across the country enriching stationers, typewriter-agencies and stenographers, not to mention the Post Office Department, wherever it went. Some escalated their "chains" from dimes to quarters, even dollars. Attempts to start $10 chains, however, got nowhere, since few could afford to gamble that amount during the depression. A typical letter bore the letterhead "Prosperity Club" and the slogan "In God We Trust," after which were printed five names with addresses and these instructions:

This chain was started in hopes of bringing you prosperity. Within three days make five copies of this letter, leaving off the top name and adding yours to the bottom, and mail or give it to five friends.

In omitting the top name send that person 10 cents. In turn as your name leaves the top, you will receive 15,625 letters with donations amounting to $1,562.50.

Now is this worth 10 cents to you? Have the faith your friend had, and this chain won't be broken.

The principle was already well known for its use in prayer-letter chains. But, as *The New Republic* observed, "it has remained . . . for the generation of Insull and Charles Mitchell, or Dr. Townsend and Huey Long, to transplant it from the drought-desiccated gardens of theology to the lush new loam of creative economics. Prayer is no longer a currency that commands wide acceptance; Colorado believes in the silver standard."[27] One Hollywood woman reportedly tried to get the City Council to pass a law making it illegal for anyone to break a chain. Some people hired boys to drop chain letters on front steps and porches. Other young boys made up letters and sold them to potential "chainers." Enterprising printing firms ran off hundreds of form letters to which only the names and addresses needed to be added. The post office in Denver, where the fad originated, found its receipts had tripled but its resources were badly strained. The volume of mail more than doubled, and at one point 100 additional clerks and carriers had to be hired, while daily deliveries were cut from three to one.[28] Individual carriers, too, found themselves strained, with *Literary Digest* observing that the chain-letter scheme had "crippled more postmen than any other game ever devised."[29] And Denver's example was soon duplicated in towns and cities from coast to coast, even in Honolulu and Havana.

Newspaper stories abounded of people who had "struck it rich" through the chain letters, further igniting the fire. Within weeks after it originated in Denver, three dollar-chain-letter "factories" sprang up in Springfield, Missouri, and $18,000 changed hands within five hours under near-riot conditions. The Associated Press reported: "Society women, waitresses, college students, taxi drivers and hundreds of others jammed downtown streets. Women shoved each other roughly in a bargain-counter rush on the chain headquarters."[30] The local newspaper reported that all other business had come to a standstill since everyone was typing up chain

letters. Three printing shops working from dawn to midnight had turned
out 40,000 of the forms and were selling them at a price of two for 15
cents (by the next day demand had driven the price up to 25 cents). Chain-
letter "exchanges," reminiscent of the stock exchange, sprang up. The
local newspaper reported: "It was a crowd of plungers, of gamblers caught
in the mad whirl of speculation that swept the city." People were
desperate to dispose of their chain letters before the urge to buy slowed
down. "In the exchanges far into the night and today, scenes rivaled those
on the floor of the New York Stock Exchange in the explosive days of
1929."[31]

The school superintendent observed:

Gambling and gamboling. There's the hope of getting something for nothing, of
course. It's closely akin to speculating on Wall Street, but I think it also has a large
element of play in it. For a long time people haven't had what they wanted; they
have been under severe restraints. Now these are suddenly loosened—not only
are they willing to take a chance, but they enjoy letting go. It's exhilarating. It's
like a game.

He was disappointed to see so many people surrendering "their minds
to the collective mind," but he expected the craze to disappear before
long. He was right.[32]

A mathematics professor calculated that the possibility of scoring on
a chain letter were doubtful. To gain the expected amount of $1,562.50
from a dime letter would, he computed, require 15,625 persons to
contribute, and a total of 244,140,625 letters would have to be circulated
for each of the original 15,625 to receive that amount. This was, of course,
double the population of the United States and would require a total of
over $24 million in dimes to pass through the mail.[33] It was, *The New
Republic* observed, a dramatic example of "the pathetic economic
cretinism that is fairly characteristic of the great masses of the American
people and alas, too often of their leaders." It was not a typical fad, like
jigsaw puzzles, but rather one that starkly revealed the "morality and
mentality of an epoch"—a period in which the credulous masses grasped
at panaceas like Huey Long and his Share Our Wealth program, or Father
Coughlin's National Union for Social Justice, or Roosevelt's juggling of
the silver price.[34]

GAMES OF CHANCE

For those who had an extra coin or more, there were other ways of
"investing" them in hopes of a return. Many people who could not afford
the price of a baseball or hockey ticket because of straitened circumstances
during the depression, managed to find an occasional nickel to feed into

the omnipresent mechanical sports games willing to swallow them. Such devices permitted players the opportunity to briefly test their skill or luck. *Business Week* found in 1933 that the popularity of such machines had brought a renaissance to the long-dormant penny arcades in the cities. Peepshow machines had, however, been pushed aside to make room for games that included mechanical baseball and other sports features, as well as new versions of bagatelle. Players who achieved the requisite scores won prizes—cameras, fountain pens, clocks, and such. Indoor amusement shops called "Sportslands" proliferated, with bagatelle machines, race horse games, miniature roulette wheels, pingpong and billiard tables, table hockey, and table golf. There were 52 Sportlands in the New York City area, inhabiting once-vacant stores, some of them earning a weekly profit of as much as $1,200. Even one in the heart of the "employment bureau district," patronized almost exclusively by unemployed men, netted a profit of around $800 per week.[35]

The urge to turn a quick profit through the investment of coins also manifested itself in the popularity of pinball games, slot machines, punchboards, and jar games. Before the onset of the depression many stores, hotels, and other businesses had refused to permit any coin games in their establishments. Hard times converted many of them, however, when it became apparent that such games could help them to pay their bills and salaries. Similarly, the desperation of the depression years undoubtedly drove many people who would ordinarily not have gambled to take a cheap stab at a sizable return.[36]

Samuel Lubell estimated that by 1939 the annual "take" from such games had reached between one-half and three-quarters of a billion dollars, which was as much as Congress had ever appropriated for the army or navy in peacetime, and twice the amount of business done in the nation's jewelry stores. Lubell estimated the capital investment in the nickel snatchers at between $20 million and $50 million, and the number of Americans dependent for all or part of their livelihood from the business at 1 million or more.[37]

Punchboards were the invention of Charles Brewer, who got the idea from attending a party where slips were drawn out of a hat. In place of a hat, Brewer substituted boards, which by the 1930s were simply sheets of cardboard with usually 1,000 holes in which tickets were fitted. For an investment of a nickel the player earned the right to punch out one of the tickets. The winning ticket usually paid $2.50, which meant that the punchboard would take in ten times the amount of the prize even when only half-punched. By 1939 the punchboard industry was using almost $500,000 worth of paper and cardboard a year in five factories, each of which could produce between 2,000 and 3,000 boards per day.[38]

Pinball games were introduced in 1932, at first in fairly simple form. Originally they involved attempts to shoot marbles into holes partially protected by pins. The instant popularity of the games, however, led many manufacturers to begin producing them, with resulting competition for new variations. Some held weekly auditions at which they reviewed the ideas of free-lance inventors. Lubell estimated that 800 manufacturers were in the business in the early years, when supply could not keep up with demand. As the craze waned later in the 1930s, the number of manufacturers shrank to one-third the earlier number and the machines grew more complicated and difficult. The pins that had guarded the holes now gave way to electric bumpers that rang bells and flashed lights on and off, and patrons received fewer marbles for their nickels. Moreover, the machines now began to resemble slot machines in that they offered jackpots and automatic payoffs, but were able to avoid prosecution because the element of skill involved set them apart from pure games of chance.[39]

Jar games, too, were a product of the 1930s, first appearing in 1933, and they quickly became almost as popular as the pinball games. For a nickel the player bought the opportunity to draw one of many four-colored tickets from a jar. If the number matched one on the jar label, the drawer could win anywhere from 10 cents to $50 or $1,000. The larger prizes could only be won, however, if the player was able to acquire three jackpot tickets. Lubell estimated that 2 million jar games had been sold between 1933 and 1938 and that another 750,000 would be sold in 1939. In the latter year the industry was keeping the factory of its inventor, Fred W. Werts, humming in Muncie, Indiana.[40] To such sorry levels had many 1920s stock market "gamblers" fallen.

LOTTERIES AND SWEEPSTAKES

Another form of the 1930s equivalent of "speculation" involved buying tickets in lotteries and sweepstakes. The Irish Sweepstakes, inaugurated in 1930, attracted thousands of American ticket buyers. Frederick Lewis Allen estimated that in 1933 (when 214 of the 2,404 winners were Americans) at least 400,000 Americans must have been ticketholders. Americans, Allen wrote, grew accustomed to "reading of janitors and unemployed chefs into whose astonished hands a hundred and fifty thousand dollars had dropped."[41] The stock "killings" of the 1920s were the sweepstakes winnings of the 1930s.

By 1936 it was estimated that $1 billion was leaving the United States every year for investment in foreign lotteries and sweepstakes. *Literary Digest* computed that it would take 16,080 stevedores, carrying 100 pounds of gold each, to load that amount of gold bullion (804 tons) aboard a ship, or, if converted to dollar bills, there would be enough to pave a 20-foot-wide highway for the 968 miles from New York City to St. Louis.[42] Such an outflow of American money was repugnant to many humanitarians and government officials at a time when the depression was causing welfare needs to burgeon despite declining tax revenues and charitable contributions. For some, the solution was obvious, and during the 1930s there were numerous advocates of state lotteries or even of a federal lottery. Religious leaders railed against such proposals, however, and all attempts to institute lotteries encountered prosecution from the Post Office Department.[43]

PARLOR GAMES

In the early 1930s contract bridge brought new excitement to that form of card playing, particularly because of the opportunity it afforded for indulging in petty gambling. Frederick Lewis Allen reported an increase in playing cards manufactured between 1930 and 1931 due to the contract bridge craze. In the latter year a match between the acknowledged experts of the game, Mr. and Mrs. Ely Culbertson on the one side, and Sidney Lenz and Oswald Jacoby on the other, attracted the kind of attention normally accorded only to college football games or heavyweight boxing matches. Favored spectators were allowed to watch from behind screens installed in the drawing room of New York's Hotel Chatham, and reporters flashed over the news wires the latest details of every novel play. The Culbertsons' victory established him as the leading authority and elevated his books on bridge to the best-seller lists. The Lynds found the game had spread by the mid-1930s down through high school to children in the sixth grade, and it had also become more popular among the working class than a decade earlier.[44]

It was estimated that a half million people were enrolled in bridge courses in 1931 and there were some 20 million involved in playing the game. No self-respecting newspaper was without a bridge column, and there were magazines and some 100 instruction books for bridge players. Elmer Davis wrote in *Harper's* in 1932 that "if contract is not the national game, it is second only to golf."[45]

If one wanted a little nickel-and-dime "action," but lacked the patience to master the intricacies of bridge playing, there was always bingo or one of its many variations—such as beano or keno—which first became really popular during the depression years. The appeal was obvious: it cost but little to play, and there was always the possibility of winning something—a ham, a tin of coffee, or perhaps a cash prize. Bingo or its variations seemed everywhere, including the home, but they came especially to be associated with church socials, despite the apparent inconsistency between churches and gambling.[46]

Others satisfied their desire to get rich quick by playing with scrip money and investing it in make-believe real estate deals as players of the major game of the 1930s. The modern version of Monopoly was invented by an unemployed Philadelphia engineer named Charles B. Darrow in 1931, using for the first board a piece of oilcloth left from the roll used to cover the kitchen table. Darrow at first sold the game only to friends and acquaintances. His attempts to interest Parker Brothers, the number-one game manufacturer in the United States, in his invention were without success. Parker was put off by the number of gadgets needed to play and the length of time (usually two hours or more) that was required to complete a game. Darrow managed to get Wanamaker's department store in Philadelphia to sell his game, however, and its popularity quickly aroused Parker's interest so that they bought the game in 1935. It quickly took the nation by storm during the 1935 Christmas season, and by early 1937 an estimated 6 million copies had already been sold. The game was also translated into seven foreign languages in its first two years, with foreign versions dealing with real estate in London, Paris, and other European cities.[47]

To even list all of the parlor games of the 1930s would be difficult, but one example, at least, should be described to illustrate their silliness. In early 1936 the popular game was one called "Sniff," which, according to the New York *Times*, had "become extremely popular within recent months, particularly as an after-dinner diversion; it is reported to have been devised by a leading stage comedienne." According to the *Times*, the game was played as follows:

A slit is made along one side of a cigarette, the tobacco is removed and the paper flattened out. Players range themselves in a circle on hands and knees and Player 1 places the cigarette paper against the end of his nose, sniffing hard. Result: the paper adheres to end of the nose. Player 2 brings his nose in juxtaposition with the cigarette paper, attempting with the aid of a sniff to transfer that paper from the nose of Player 1 to his own.

And so on around the circle.[48]

The depression also saw a craze for prize contests, with newspaper and magazine readers, and radio listeners, urged by interested advertisers to complete advertising slogans for them, or to solve contests, in exchange for which they could win prizes—automobiles, trips, perhaps a year's supply of the manufacturer's product. And, for people with more leisure time than many of them wanted, it was also a decade that saw the flowering of hobbies, with department stores creating hobby departments, and newspapers and magazines carrying hobby sections. Roosevelt's well-known hobby of collecting stamps stimulated others to take up that pursuit.[49]

MINIATURE GOLF

One of the first and most fleeting fads of the 1930s was miniature golf. Golf had, of course, been for some time a diversion of the middle class and well-off, played on rolling and well-landscaped courses distant from the urban centers. Miniature golf presented a smaller-scale, lower-cost, and local version of the sport of the "swells."

First established in Tennessee in 1927 by a real estate operator named Garnet Carter, the industry quickly spread throughout the United States after northern tourists were exposed to it in Florida. Almost any good-sized vacant lot was adequate for a modest course and, as Frederick Lewis Allen wrote, "hundreds of thousands of Americans were . . . earnestly knocking golf balls along cottonseed greenswards, through little mouse holes in wooden barricades, over little bridges, and through drainpipes, while the proprietors of these new playgrounds listened happily to the tinkle of the cash register."[50]

In 1930, the first year of the depression, it was estimated that $150 million was invested in courses and that some $225 million was being spent annually by players. The industry briefly provided employment for 200,000 workers and breathed temporary life into the steel, concrete, and sporting goods industries.[51] Courses could be constructed in a week at a cost of about $2,000. In one single week more than 5,000 courses were laid out, and for a brief time during the peak of the craze there were 22 miniature golf courses within a radius of four blocks in New York City.[52] In January 1931 the Department of Commerce reported that miniature golf had become a $125 million industry; but as with all fads this one flashed brightly and, then, like a meteor, burnt itself out, leaving most of the courses to be reclaimed once again by weeds by the end of the year.

CAMPUS FADS

Some of the more interesting fads or crazes of the 1930s originated on college campuses, where students tended to be as imaginative and outrageous as in the 1920s. One of the college movements of the 1930s was a parody on the demands of World War I veterans for immediate full payment of their "bonuses"—the amount due them at the end of their government endowment life insurance policies—instead of waiting for the policies to mature. In 1935, Lewis J. Gorin, Jr., of Louisville, Kentucky, founded the Veterans of Future Wars among government majors at Princeton University. Their manifesto read:

Whereas it is inevitable that this country will be engaged in war within the next thirty years, and whereas it is by all accounts likely that every man of military age will have a part in this war, we therefore demand that the government make known its intention to pay an adjusted service compensation, sometimes called a bonus, of $1,000 to every male citizen between the ages of 18 and 36, said bonus to be payable the first of June 1965. Furthermore, we believe a study of history demonstrates that it is customary to pay all bonuses before they are due. Therefore, we demand immediate cash payment, plus 3 per cent interest compounded annually and retroactively from the first of June 1965, to the first of June 1935. It is but common right that this bonus be paid now, for many will be killed and wounded in the next war, and hence they, the most deserving, will not otherwise get the full benefit of their country's gratitude.

Within ten days after this manifesto was released, the movement swelled across the country and by the end of March 1936 there were 120 college chapters from coast to coast, as well as many outside of colleges, with a paid membership of over 6,000. The movement eventually expanded to include girls of the Gold Star Mothers of Future Wars, "who expect to lose sons in the next war," and Chaplains of Future Wars, organized among divinity students. The salute of the Veterans of Future Wars was the right arm held out, palm up.[53]

For one newspaper, the movement was not only "a lampoon on the importunity of veterans pressing for bonuses and pensions," but also "a satire on the stupidities presented in the war psychology." But the movement did not stop there. It broadened to include satires of two other movements current during the New Deal years when some of its members also demanded $200 per month revolving pensions for future veterans (the Townsend Plan) and a 30-hour workweek for them![54]

Then, late in the 1930s, there was the well-known goldfish-swallowing craze on college campuses. The fad apparently began in early March 1939, when a Harvard freshman named Lothrop Withington, Jr. won a $10 bet by swallowing a live goldfish in front of 100 classmates. When the word spread, no campus, it seemed, was to be outdone by any other. A junior at Franklin and Marshall College was apparently next, in swallowing three, but that feat was soon dwarfed by a sophomore at Harvard who reclaimed honor for The Yard by swallowing an apparently unsurmountable total of 24. Thereafter the totals mounted until by the end of March the record was up to 67 and doctors were warning of the dangers of tapeworm and anemia.[55]

Humor, too, went through its fads in the 1930s, and many of them originated on high school or college campuses. In the early 1930s Americans got laughs by going around shouting "Where's Elmer?" The craze apparently was born in 1931 at an American Legion convention in Detroit, when a delegate named Elmer didn't show up and his fellow Legionnaires broadcast their search for him. Then high school and college students turned to telling "Little Audrey" stories and playing Handies, a "What's This?" game.

The most notable, and durable, of the fads in humor was, however, the "knock-knock" joke of the middle of the decade, which was even made into a hit song. Tradition has it that this "nonsense craze" originated among college students worried about their exams, though exactly where it began was disputed. A typical "knock-knock" went:

Knock! Knock!
Who's there?
Delia.
Delia who?
Delia cards off the top.

Or:

Knock! Knock!
Who's there?
Tarzan.
Tarzan who?
Tarzan stripes forever.

Or:

Knock! Knock!
Who's there?
Freda.
Freda who?
Freda you; ten dollars to everybody else.

Tired of listening to knock-knock jokes, orchestra leader Vincent Lopez and his drummer wrote a song about them in hopes that it would put an end to the fad. The song, however, became a hit and spread the knock-knock joke to the most remote reaches of the United States. Each time the song was played new knock-knock jokes were used. Lopez offered prizes for new knock-knock jokes and received 5,000 letters full of them. Newspapers, too, began to award cash prizes for them. One newspaper writer referred to the craze for knock-knock as "a devastating mania and a mental disease," while *Literary Digest* referred to it as "America's newest nonsense craze."[56]

Another "nonsense craze" of the mid-1930s was that for paper masks, which flared up briefly like the other fads of the decade and then died out. The masks were made up in likenesses of famous characters—historic figures, movie stars, even cartoon characters. For a few cents one could escape into a different persona like Abraham Lincoln, Krazy Kat, or Greta Garbo, for a few hours. Parties were held at which masks were worn. A staggering total of 30 million were sold, suggesting that nearly that many people must have donned one at some time—approximately one-fourth of the American population, or one-third of all adults. The "mental result," wrote the New York *Times*, was that "each of those millions ceased for a moment to be his or her own weary self; the self was not merely effaced but made into a recognizable and adulated notability."[57]

PHOTOGRAPHY

The purchase and use of cameras assumed the dimensions of a fad during the 1930s, triggered in part, perhaps, by the growing use of photographs in newspapers and magazines, including the popularity of new magazines like *Life*, which were devoted almost exclusively to candid photographs. Technological advances also helped, including the development of more sensitive film and the use of flashbulbs for night photography. Cheap plastic cameras, really little more than toys but capable of good results, sold in large numbers at prices between 39 and 50 cents. Their success inspired Eastman Kodak to introduce in 1934 the Baby Brownie, a plastic box camera that took pictures double the size of the "toys" and sold for $1.

The real fad within photography during the 1930s was, however, an unlikely one for a nation in the midst of a depression. It was the growing popularity of expensive 35mm "miniature" cameras, or "minicams," largely German imports with names like Leica, Voightlander, and Rolleiflex. The new fad meant that the average price paid for a camera, which had fallen steadily between 1920 and 1931, actually rose sharply in the depression years of 1932 and 1933. These cameras took postage-stamp sized pictures on fine-grain film that stood up to the enlargement that was required. They were popular with serious photographers because they were handy and offered a wide choice of lenses and films. *Business Week* found professionals and amateur camera nuts "cheerfully" paying "the price of a good used car" for the new cameras and the gadgets, like exposure meters at $35 each, that went with them.[58]

In the second half of the 1930s, two of the most popular Christmas gifts for men were items that were new products of the decade. Sixteen-millimeter motion picture cameras and other equipment for the amateur moviemaker were already available when the 1930s began, but the early models were bulky and expensive. In 1932, Eastman Kodak introduced the Cine-Kodak Eight, an 8-millimeter camera that exposed only half of a roll of 16-millimeter film at a time and quadrupled the amount of movie that could be shot on a given length of film. This made possible a smaller camera that could shoot on a 25-foot roll of film the same four minutes of projection time as a larger camera containing 100 feet of film. The result was both a cheaper camera and lower film cost. The Cine-Kodak Eight sold for $29.50, while a complete outfit, including projector, cost $52. A 25-foot roll of film cost of $2.25, about one-third of the price of the equivalent 100-foot roll for a conventional 16mm camera.[59]

This, however, was only the beginning. In 1935, RCA introduced the first amateur sound-on-film movie camera, weighing less than nine pounds fully equipped with lights. *Scientific American* reported that in "appearance and size it differs only slightly from the silent amateur movie camera." The sound cameras quickly found numerous practical applications.

Dr. Kurt Lewin, professor of child psychology at Cornell, used them to film children from hidden locations so that their reactions to commands, suggestions, and other stimuli could be recorded for later analysis by interested psychologists. The federal government was also a customer, using the cameras to document soil erosion and to record assistance to distressed vessels at sea by the Coast Guard.[60]

DRY SHAVING

Another popular Christmas gift that took much of the country by storm late in the decade was the electric razor, or "dry razor" as they were referred to in the 1930s. The dry shaver was invented by Colonel Jacob Schick, a Spanish-American War and World War I veteran, who had been born in Ottumwa, Iowa. After retiring from the army, Schick turned to inventing and searched for a product that would be needed by all men. After getting patents for a pencil sharpener and for the Schick Injector Razor, Schick used the money to perfect the electric razor, for which he got his first patents in 1928. In 1931 he opened his first factory in a Stamford, Connecticut, loft where, with a dozen employees, he began making the first Schick electric razors by hand and selling them for $25. He sold about 3,000 of them the first year, and thereafter tripled sales every year (except 1934) until 1939. By the latter year he was selling over 750,000 electric razors per year at $15 apiece and taking in $7.5 million.[61]

During the 1930s, while Schick fought infringements of his patents, the competition grew. From a monopoly of electric shaver sales, Schick's share of the market had fallen to approximately 50 percent by 1939, when 1.5 million were sold for approximately $20 million. By this time they had begun to offer serious competition to the "wet shaving" industry. So popular had dry shaving become that hotels, railroads, and luxury liners were forced to install convenient 110-volt outlets for their use in rooms and Pullman compartments. One enterprising Cadillac dealer installed electric shavers on the dashboard of his cars to spur sales. For those who expected to be away from the convenience of electricity there were portable razors with batteries good for up to three months of shaving.[62]

Some of the electric razors were marketed in deluxe models with gold-plated shaving heads, colored cases (made from bakelite), and fancy boxes. Some offered attachments, including one that could be used for massaging the gums. Remington Rand even marketed a model with a transparent case so that owners could watch the motor operate. Most electric razors were sold in the 1930s through credit jewelry stores where they might be purchased for as little as 25 cents per week on installments—not much more than the weekly cost of wet shaving. The jewelers profited, also, from the purchases that men frequently made of watches or jewelry during their weekly visits to make the payments on their shavers.[63]

CHAPTER THREE

Comics and Popular Literature

COMIC STRIPS

Comic strips did not originate in the 1930s, having begun in American newspapers in the 1890s. From the very beginning, "comic" strip was a misnomer since many of the strips featured adventure or took the form of mild soap operas. The strips burgeoned during the 1910s and 1920s and reading them became a ritual for Americans, especially on Sundays.

Some of the most durable strips, however, originated in the 1930s. On the humorous side, Blondie began in 1930, L'il Abner in 1934, and two Walt Disney characters made the transition from movies to comics in 1930 (Mickey Mouse) and 1936 (Donald Duck). The decade was more notable, however, for its adventure strips. Buck Rogers brought science fiction to the comics in 1929, and was soon joined by Flash Gordon in that genre. The jungle, too, exerted an appeal for Americans seeking escape from the realities of the depression, with the popularity of features like Tarzan and Jungle Jim. Crime strips mirrored the popularity of that theme in radio and the movies, beginning with Dick Tracy and then by a variety of crime fighters who possessed superhuman powers: Mandrake the Magician, the Phantom, Superman, Batman, Wonder Woman, and others. Readers could also escape into history with Prince Valliant, and to exotic places with Terry and the Pirates.

Slapstick violence had always characterized even the humorous strips, but the action strips that proliferated during the 1930s featured it on a larger and more serious scale. Some bemoaned the trend and saw it as indicative of an ominous historical movement. The violence of the comic strips, the *Saturday Review (SR)* opined, mirrored (and in fact preceded) the growing violence in the real world, such as could be seen in Germany and Italy. The strips were "an index to the times." Moreover, the comics had shown, for at least 20 years, a "trend against democracy." The "essence of their humor" was in "making a monkey out of the everyday, common-place man who is the backbone of democracy," *SR* wrote. The average man had been portrayed as the "most undignified, least to be respected, most inconsiderable of human beings in history." Not since the writings of Scott and Shakespeare had there been demonstrated such a "satisfaction in the contemptible commonness and incapacity of the common man." Violence, *SR* wrote, had taken "the place of the humanitarianism which thirty years ago would have had little children reading stories of boys and girls who were successful because they were kind and good," and "a tolerant contempt for the average man has ousted a spread-eagle faith in the democracy."[1]

The trend was, however, true not only of the comic strips but of American humor in general. As Gilbert Seldes pointed out, early American humor had glorified the common sense of the common man and had been directed "against all pretensions of the superior." By the 1930s, however, much of American humor had become "sophisticated," in that it now pointed out the "stupidities of the stupid" without devoting the attention to the "stupidity of the intelligent" that was the essence of satire. The open-mouthed farmer gaping at the tall buildings of the city, Seldes pointed out, was in no way inferior to the "stupidity of the city man when confronted with a cow," and yet it was the former that was being stressed by the "sophisticated" humorists of the 1930s.[2]

The popularity of even Mickey Mouse stemmed not so much from humor as the way he dealt with life, according to one critic, who wrote that Mickey was "like a Henry James American among a bunch of continentals: the fine simplicity of his logic out-subtles all the professional serpents, and he comes home generally without the bacon [but] with self-respect intact." Moreover, Mickey was like a one-mouse melting pot, a blend of America's many civilizations, drawing on the virtues of each. As jazz represented the miscegenation of music, Mickey represented the miscegenation of art.[3]

Liberal journals like *The Nation* and *The New Republic* concentrated their fire on one particular comic strip in the 1930s. Harold Gray's Little Orphan Annie had been around since 1924 and ten years later was widely syndicated to some 135 daily and 100 Sunday newspapers. It was not Annie who drew their fire, although she was dismissed ungallantly as "none-too-bright" by *The Nation*, but her guardian, Oliver "Daddy" Warbucks, who seemed in the mid-1930s to be occupying more and more of the strip. Gray's portrayal of Warbucks as an altruistic businessman, whose efforts to bring benefits to the people were continually sabotaged by unscrupulous rivals working through pliant politicians (one of whom bore a striking resemblance to the liberal Senator George Norris of Nebraska) and by self-serving labor union organizers, brought cries of "Hooverism" and "Fascism in the Funnies" from *The New Republic*. Orphan Annie, wrote Richard Neuberger, the "red-headed idol of thousands of children," was "doing heroic service in the cause of Andrew W. Mellon, Samuel Insull and other persecuted philanthropists."[4] Readers of the strip were being taught "that all reform legislation of the Roosevelt administration, and all attempts to extend union organization, were no more than the tricks of one set of capitalists to ruin another set," and that "those who now rule industry are good and kindly, and that their rivals are evil."[5]

The New Republic applauded the decision of the Huntington (West Virginia) *Herald-Dispatch* to drop the strip, while *The Nation*, after describing Annie herself as "stupid" and "impressionable and dull," similarly revealed its commitment to freedom of speech by wondering why "such a respectable family newspaper as the liberal Baltimore *Sun* should allow the outfit to run loose in its pages."[6] No doubt the fact that the strip was syndicated by the Chicago *Tribune* and Hearst syndicates, two New Deal opponents, contributed to the hostility of both liberal journals.

Such criticism did not, however, lessen Annie's appeal to her readers, and she remained, as one source observed, "an important symbol for the Depression years." Although she did not appear in any animated films during the 1930s, Little Orphan Annie did have the distinction of spawning two live-action movies: one in 1932 and the other in 1939. There were also Little Orphan Annie Little Big Books and a variety of Little Orphan Annie toys and games.[7]

If *The Nation* and *The New Republic* appeared to have lost their sense of humor in the 1930s, so did the comic strips. For a time in that decade, wrote Frank Luther Mott, "humor seemed about to drop out of the strips," though it had begun to creep back in by 1940.[8] In bemoaning the potential influence of Daddy Warbucks, however, the two liberal magazines were undoubtedly aware of studies that showed the comic strips were more interesting to newspaper readers than any other features and than most news. As a consequence, when features had to be cut because of red ink, it was usually the comics that were the last to go.[9] They were, one observer wrote, "America's day-dream," a "sort of still movie."[10] In at least one part of the newspaper Americans could find escape from the news.

President Roosevelt, himself, made an appearance in one comic strip during the 1930s. Cartoonist Ham Fisher wrote his character, boxer Joe Palooka, into a predicament in mid-1938. Palooka had become a member of the French Foreign Legion and Fisher could find no way to extricate him. The only solution seemed to be intervention by the president of the United States. An appeal to the White House brought Roosevelt's permission for Fisher to use him in the strip. Knobby Walsh, Palooka's manager, thereupon traveled to the White House in the strip, received a letter from Roosevelt to the president of France requesting Palooka's discharge, and Fisher's hero was free for new adventures.[11]

In an era of standardization of newspapers, one feature that differentiated a newspaper from its competitors was its particular array of comics. The most successful newspaper in any given city in the early 1930s, Robert Benchley observed, was likely to be the one that carried the popular syndicated comic strip of those years, The Gumps.[12]

COMIC BOOKS

The 1930s spawned three unique offshoots from the comic strips. One of these was the comic book. The first modern comic book, in the now familiar 7½ × 10 inch size printed in color with a glossy cover, was *Funnies on Parade*, which, like the first jigsaw puzzles, was a promotional giveaway—in this case by Procter and Gamble—in 1933. As with jigsaw puzzles, the popularity of the giveaway suggested money-making possibilities, and the next year the first commercial comic book was released, *Famous Funnies*, which was made up, however, of reprints of newspaper comic strips. Copies of *Famous Funnies*, too, were quickly snapped up and the comic book industry was born. The first comic book containing all new material was published in 1935, and it was soon followed by a variety of others in the late 1930s, including *Detective Comics* and *Action Comics* (in which Superman made his debut). The success of Superman quickly spawned numerous imitators including Batman, Captain America, and Wonder Woman.

The second contribution of the 1930s was the Big Little Book, now long forgotten by, or unknown to, most Americans. These were hardbound books approximately 1'' thick by 4'' wide and 4½'' tall, designed to fit the hands and lunchboxes of children, with large-print text on the left page and comic illustrations on the right, that sold for 10 or 15 cents, sometimes less in smaller versions. The books were the brainchild of Samuel Lowe, president of Whitman Publishing Company, who marketed the first one, *The Adventures of Dick Tracy*, in 1933. The following year Lowe negotiated a contract with Walt Disney Studios for the rights to produce books featuring Disney characters, and Mickey Mouse brought the Big Little Books to the counters of all the major chain stores. Big Little Books thereafter covered virtually every subject area from fairy tales to pirate, cowboy, and detective adventures, and even versions of the classics, as well as all of the major comic strip characters.[13] Some of them had small illustrations in the upper right-hand corner, each of them slightly different from that on the previous page, so that when flipped they gave the illusion of movement like an animated film.

Another feature of the 1930s was the "pop-up" series of children's books, which gave comic strip characters and others a three-dimensional aspect. Beginning in 1932, the pop-up books offered Little Orphan Annie, Disney characters, Dick Tracy, Buck Rogers, and others in action scenes that popped up when the books opened.[14]

THE PULPS

Not much above the level of the comics, if at all, were the popular pulp magazines of the 1930s. Cheap magazines were, of course, ideal for a depressed America in which people had the time for recreation and a desire to seal themselves off at least temporarily from reality, but little money to spend. The result was an explosion of new titles in the pulp magazine industry during the decade, with the themes following those that were popular in the other media: detective and mystery titles, westerns, adventures, and even science fiction. The most "notable and memorable" development in the 1930s, says one scholar, was the rebirth of the "hero novel," which had been so important in the industry in the 1890s. These featured crime-fighters like The Shadow and Nick Carter, World War I heroes like Lone Eagle, and G-8 and His Battle Aces, master spies like Secret Agent "X" and Operator #5, and Western heroes like Masked Rider. So popular were the new hero pulps that a new one debuted every two months between January 1933 and April 1935, and the pace did not slacken during the remainder of the decade. The pulps attracted some first-class writers, including Edgar Rice Burroughs, Zane Grey, Dashiell Hammett, Raymond Chandler, Erle Stanley Gardner, Rex Stout, and dozens of others.[15]

The popularity of the pulps can be seen in the figures released by one of their major publishers in 1935. A. A. Wyn reported that each year 125 pulp titles produced 2,000 carloads of magazines that were read by 10 million fans. Annually $500,000 worth of art and engravings as well as 1.5 million worth of manuscripts were printed at a cost of $2 million on $1,250,000 worth of paper.[16] And the success of the pulps was all the more remarkable because they relied so little on advertising revenue. The success or failure of a pulp magazine, then, depended almost totally on the support of its readers, readers who were drawn for the most part from the working class. For that reason, the literature of the pulps was a better reflection of the taste and intellectual level of their audience than was the case with other magazines, and that literature was "almost entirely a literature of violence (in the Western story magazines and the innumerable crime magazines) and of sickly and even morbid sentiment in the romantic publications for women."[17]

The emergence and popularity in the "lowbrow literature" of the 1930s of brutality, violence, and perversion was disquieting for some. When taken in combination with the popularity of the confession and astrology magazines among lower class families, it added up to "an appalling picture of working-class culture." On the positive side, however, was the popularity of such magazines as *Popular Mechanics* and *Popular Science*, as well as the outdoor and sports magazines, with working-class readers.[18] In her travels across the country, Maxine Davis found the boys and girls reading mainly cheap magazines like *Western Stories, War Aces, Love Story, True Story, Movie*, and *Detective*, with occasionally a *Popular Mechanics* or *Popular Science*.[19]

If chuckles were rare in the comic strips of the 1930s, Americans could turn to pulp humor magazines for a good laugh. At the beginning of the 1930s, the reigning example of this genre was *Captain Billy's Whiz Bang*, a product of the 1920s. By the early 1930s, however, its circulation had dropped, and when Dell introduced *Ballyhoo* in 1931, *Whiz Bang* disappeared from the scene. *Ballyhoo* turned out to be, however, more in the nature of the fads of the 1930s than a permanent institution. After reaching a peak circulation of 2 million copies it fizzled out after two years. Its initial success, though, says Theodore Peterson, "sent competitors hurrying to slap together imitations; it begat 'Ballyhoo" dresses, neckties, scarves, rings, cuff links, scarf pins, games, songs, greeting cards, and night clubs, and its editor wrote a musical show named Ballyhoo which had some of the success of its namesake." The magazine died in 1939.[20] For most of the decade, however, it had furnished, Clifton Fadiman wrote, "a rowdy and scatalogical subject matter" that afforded "particular delight to the most constipated nation on earth."[21]

For those whose tastes went beyond even the risqué humor of *Ballyhoo*, there were numerous purveyors of bawdier humor and nudity during the depression years. Many of these latter were marketed ostensibly for the "art lover" and photography fan. Among the titles available on newsstands in the 1930s were *Art Lover's Magazine, Nudist, Hi-Jinks, Snappy Stories, Cupid's Capers, Jim Jam Jems, French Stories, Nifty Stories*, and *Wild Cherries*. The 1930s also saw periodic attempts to suppress the sale of such "pornographic" material, and in 1936 two publishers were fined and sentenced to three months in jail for engaging in interstate commerce of them.[22]

In the same category as the hero pulps were the true confession magazines. *True Story*, begun in 1919, had attained a circulation of 2 million by 1926 and its success quickly began to spawn imitators. *Modern Romances* was launched in 1930, and as confession magazines became a staple of women's reading during the depression others followed, including *Secrets* in 1936 and *Personal Romances* in 1937. Presumably women obtained the same sort of satisfaction from reading such magazines as they did from listening to radio soap operas during the 1930s.[23] Clifton Fadiman found them pandering "almost entirely to elementary sexual cravings and the *voyeur* tendency which seeks to bathe in the life confessions of one's neighbors."[24] An offshoot of the confession magazines was the factual detective magazine that originated in the 1920s and proliferated during the 1930s. Scores of the genre debuted in the 1930s, most notably *True Detective Mysteries* and *Official Detective Stories*, both established in 1934.[25]

MAGAZINES FOR ALL INTERESTS

The 1930s also saw the birth of the first general-interest men's magazine. Previous to this time, magazines directed toward the male audience had been specialized, on such subjects as sports, hunting and fishing, or home craftsmanship. Some of these were born during the 1930s, as for example *Sports Illustrated*, which first appeared in 1935. The first magazine to direct itself at the more general interests of men was *Esquire*, which originated in 1933. It was, however, high-priced (at 50 cents per issue) for the depression years, and it emphasized quality fiction, fashion, and costly artwork—much of it in color—that narrowed its appeal to mainly upper-class men. By contrast, *True Magazine*, which appeared in 1936, was more appealing to the average male because of its mixture of adventure, sports, science, and personalities, and its lower price.[26]

Women's magazines were plentiful before the 1930s, but new ones sprouted during that decade. Whereas the trend in men's magazines was away from the specific and toward the general, the trend in women's magazines was the reverse, with new magazines exploiting particular themes. On the theory that women got married in both good times and bad, Wells Drorbaugh launched *Bride's Magazine* in 1934. The following year, Street & Smith introduced *Mademoiselle*, designed for women in the 17 to 30 age range, and it quickly became a lucrative venture. In April 1939, Condé Nast brought out *Glamour*, a little sister of the older *Vogue*, which was likewise designed for young women—especially young working women.[27] Another popular theme of the 1930s was family life and child-rearing. *Parents' Magazine* began the trend when it debuted in 1929, and its commercial success encouraged others to enter the field. *Baby Talk* appeared in 1935, and it was followed by numerous others. *Boys' and Girls' Newspaper* was the first of numerous magazines that were designed for boys or girls or both. The *Journal of Living* began in 1935, designed by the Serutan Company to appeal mainly to people over 40.

The older women's magazines, meanwhile, gained in circulation during the 1930s. By 1938 the combined circulation of the five leading women's magazines—including *Good Housekeeping, McCall's, Pictorial Review, Women's Home Companion,* and *Ladies' Home Journal*—had climbed to about 13 million. Robert Cantwell wrote:

With their recurring articles on how to keep a budget, how to make your own clothes, how to conceal the wear in old chairs, restore old pictures, paint shabby walls, make a tasty meal of left-overs, and glue together furniture that is falling apart—with all this practical and pathetic advice, the women's magazines seem to be run by people who know what shape the middle-class is in.

In this respect, they contrasted with magazines like *The Saturday Evening Post*, whose editors seemed to be unaware of, or determined to ignore, those realities.[28]

The 1930s also saw the beginnings of grocery market women's magazines. The A & P Stores began in the early 1930s to distribute a free leaflet called the "A & P Menu Sheet," which gave housewives pointers on how to shop for food bargains during the depression and menus for preparing low-cost meals. The leaflet became so popular, reaching a distribution of nearly 800,000 by 1937, that A & P converted it in that year to a magazine named *Woman's Day*. The new magazine was sold only in A & P stores and for only 3 cents per copy. Meanwhile, *Family Circle* was inaugurated in 1932 as a giveaway tabloid weekly that contained articles about food, fashions, beauty, movies, and radio. It was available only on the counters of 1,275 grocery chain stores, including Safeway and Red Owl.[29]

The growing popularity of radio and movies in the 1930s likewise spawned an increase in fan magazines for both. The 1930s, for example, saw the beginnings of *Modern Screen* and *Movies*, both in 1930, *Movie Mirror* and *Romantic Movie Stories*, both in 1933, and *Movie Life* in 1937. According to one critic, the movie fan magazines were a respected medium until the mid-1930s, when publishers began aiming at a younger audience and sought sensational revelations about the stars to attract them. The rise and popularity of radio fan magazines was aided by a decision of the newspapers in the early 1930s to stop publishing program schedules, which they had been doing for free, except as paid advertising. Among those that began in the 1930s were *Radio Guide* and *Radio Mirror*.[30]

Fads of the 1930s also spawned new magazines. The growing interest in amateur photography that was associated with the new "candid" 35mm cameras of the decade produced three new magazines in the late 1930s: *Popular Photography, Modern Photography*, and *U.S. Camera*. The popularity of skiing in the 1930s likewise produced *Ski* magazine beginning in 1935. Other fad-related magazines appeared in the 1930s, many of them as short-lived as the fads themselves.

Associated with the new interest in photography, both as cause and effect, was the popularity of photo journalism magazines like *Life*, which appeared in November 1936. The success of *Life* stimulated others to enter the field of magazines devoted largely to photographs. Some of these were short-lived, but one successful competitor in the 1930s was *Look* magazine, which appeared in January 1937, just two months after *Life* began publication. Its purpose, the first issue proclaimed, was to give its readers "a thousand eyes to see round the world."[31] "In the wake of *Life* and *Look*, millions of copies of picture magazines poured onto the newstands as other publishers introduced their entries," Peterson wrote. "The mortality rate was high, but during 1937 and 1938 new ones hopefully appeared almost as fast as the failures disappeared." These new, often short-lived entries, did not devote themselves to the news, like *Life*, but often purveyed mainly "sex and sensation." Among the competitors were *Photo-History, Peek, Now and Then, Foto, Picture*, and *Click*. The latter, especially, promoted themes of "sex and shock," and was often barely above the level of the earlier-mentioned magazines for "art-lovers." *Click*'s principal competition in cheesecake came from *Pic*, which was launched in 1937, and featured "photographs of young women not far removed from nudity."[32]

Studies showed that the typical American bought and read few books—far fewer than people in the advanced countries of Europe—but observers concluded that Americans probably spent more time reading than their European counterparts. Their reading, however, consisted mainly of popular magazines and newspapers, even if many of them read only the comics in the latter. "The deficit in book sales," Elmer Davis concluded, was "partly compensated by the immense circulation of magazines."[33] In 1938 there were an estimated 1,200 weekly magazines with a circulation of around 50 million and some 2,000 monthly magazines going to approximately 100 million buyers. While the number of magazines declined during the depression, the number of magazine readers grew. The circulation of the pulp magazines, alone, grew from 8 million to 14 million between 1928 and 1938.[34] As these magazines seemed to try, at least, to appeal to every sort of taste, any American who wanted to read could find something in them that would suit him. But, one critic observed, the magazines of the 1930s presented "essentially a literature, not of inquiry, but of distraction, a literature least of all calculated to provoke questions or excite controversy."[35]

OPINION MAGAZINES

The debate over the new direction of American liberalism was joined in opinion magazines in the 1930s. Liberal magazines like *The Nation* and *The New Republic* for the most part championed the new direction, with some dissenting articles, and copies could be found on many desks in Washington. Outside of Washington, however, their combined circulation of perhaps 75,000 was spread rather thinly over the breadth of America (moreover, Robert Cantwell observed, when the circulation of one increased, that of the other declined). Other brief-lived magazines were occasionally even more radical, like *Ken*, or the *Modern Monthly*, which predicted a proletarian revolution for 1937. These liberal and radical journals peaked in circulation in 1931, then lost nearly half their circulation the following year, hit bottom in 1934, and only climbed slightly from 1935 onward.[36]

There was no equivalent ideological journal presenting conservative ideas, a fact lamented by columnist Mark Sullivan, who despaired at the volume of unanswered propaganda in behalf of the radical changes that were being proposed.[37] In soliciting an essay from Wall Street banker Thomas Lamont to answer the attacks, *Saturday Review* editor Bernard DeVoto pointed out that "capitalism has a low name in the literary world these days," in part because the "attack is always more attractive than the defense," and "people who can speak with authority about the workings of the capitalist system have neglected or perhaps even declined to write about it."[38] Business journals like *Business Week* and *Nation's Business* naturally championed their position but were little read outside the business community.

The most influential magazine on the conservative side was probably *The Saturday Evening Post* of George Horace Lorimer, which regularly attacked the New Deal in editorials and articles, though as one observer noted, those attacks seemed "out of place in the midst of good-natured fiction whose point invariably is that everything is going to turn out all right."[39] In circulation and readership it far outstripped all radical/liberal magazines combined, but with the exception of Lorimer's anti-New Deal editorials and occasional articles critical of the administration, the *Post* was a magazine for entertainment, not ideological debate, and most readers bought it for its fiction and amusing and helpful articles rather than for its point of view on politics. *Liberty* and *Collier's* were the two principal competitors of the *Post* for the middle-class audience, and all three, Clifton Fadiman observed snobbishly, published "nothing unsuited to the intelligence of a fourteen-year-old."[40] However, all three grew immensely in circulation during the 1930s, the *Post* by perhaps 1 million, *Liberty* some 800,000, and *Collier's* by 1.3 million.[41]

THE SATURDAY EVENING POST

James Playsted Wood gives one example of the influence of *The Saturday Evening Post*. In 1934 it published a series of articles on the struggles with poverty of a young teacher at her school in the Tennessee hills. Wood wrote:

Though no solicitation was made, gifts of money, clothes, books, and other equipment poured into the *Post* from every part of the country for transmission to the teacher. To handle the enormous correspondence which resulted from the articles, the magazine had to employ an assistant for the article writer and a secretary for the schoolteacher. The . . . school received everything it needed, and so much more that arrangements were made to direct the continuing flow of gifts to schools in other mountain villages.[42]

The *Post* had a circulation of 3 million by 1937 and was, Wood says, "virtually without a competitor as the largest weekly." It was "seen and read everywhere," and its "influence mounted continually."[43] One must assume, therefore, that its fiction was among the most widely read in America and its fiction writers among the most popular and influential.

Curiously enough, however, the name of Clarence Buddington Kelland is rarely mentioned, if at all, in studies of the fiction of the 1930s, although writers of fiction are regularly discussed in college literature classes whose works were probably not read by as many people in the entire decade as one Kelland short story or novel segment attracted in a single week. In the three years between August 1932 and August 1935 alone, Kelland published in the *Post* a dozen single-issue short stories, and six novels serialized in another 36 issues. In sum, Kelland's writings appeared in nearly one-third of the issues of the *Post* during those three years, or an average of over once per month. But Kelland's literary output was not limited to the *Post*. During those same three years he published eight short stories and the first two segments of a novel in *Ladies Home Journal*, a novel and over a dozen stories in *American Mercury*, and two short stories in *Collier's*!

MENCKEN ON THE 1930s

Besides the *Post*'s occasional acerbic editorials on the subject of the New Deal, the *American Mercury* also waged a fairly constant war on Roosevelt and the New Deal, even after H. L. Mencken departed as editor in 1933. Mencken, especially, pilloried Roosevelt and the New Dealers with a vengeance and a vocabulary unmatched by anyone in the 1930s. Roosevelt's mind, Mencken wrote soon after the 1932 election, "performs its operations in a sort of pink and perfumed fog."[44] Three years into the Roosevelt presidency, Mencken wrote:

Quacks are always friendly and ingratiating fellows, and not infrequently their antics are very amusing. The Hon. Franklin D. Roosevelt, LL.D., is typical of the species. There has never been a more amiable President, not even excepting the Martyr Harding, and there has never been a better showman, not even excepting T. Roosevelt.

The New Deal had begun "with a din of alarming blather about the collapse of capitalism, the ruin of the Republic, and the imminence of revolution," and now claimed to have averted all of these calamities. In fact, the situation had not been "a tenth as bad as the patient was induced to believe, and the medicines administered . . . were almost wholly fraudulent and ineffective." If the country was now in better condition it was not because of the New Deal, but in spite of it.[45]

As for the people around Roosevelt, Mencken wrote, they had been "obscure and impotent fellows who flushed with pride when they got a nod from the cop at the corner," suddenly raised by FDR to "the secular rank of princes of the blood, and the ghostly faculties of cardinal archbishops." Compared to their rags-to-riches stories, those of Hollywood waitresses who achieved overnight stardom paled to insignificance. Not surprisingly, he found, those elevated from nowhere to such power and position found it difficult to keep their heads.[46]

In 1939, after six years of the New Deal, Mencken concluded that it had been "a gigantic flop." The billions of dollars spent to encourage economic recovery "might as well have been laid out for toy balloons or lollypops." The only beneficiaries were "the huge hordes of job-holders who now snuggle at the public teat." The New Dealers, he repeated, were all, "with a few lonely exceptions, complete nonentities—professional uplifters, third-rate lawyers, chronic job-holders, decayed chautauquans, and the like. The one criterion that seems to have been applied to them is the criterion of incompetence." Not even Harding's administration had "brought together a more forbidding gang of quacks and shysters. . . . After six years in office they are twice as imbecile as they were when they began."[47]

Mencken, however, lacked the following that he had attracted in the 1920s, even though his attacks were as incisive as ever and the direction of those attacks was unchanged. Mencken had always criticized whatever administration occupied the White House, even those he had voted for, so there was no reason for Roosevelt to be an exception. Mencken had also waged a continual war against do-gooders and similar quacks, and the Roosevelt administration was filled with them, so they were a ready target. And Mencken had always regarded the average American "homo boobien" with contempt. Now the support of the majority of Americans for Roosevelt was only proof that he had been right all along about them. What affected Mencken's appeal was the changed circumstances of the 1930s. In the 1920s Mencken had been regarded as antiestablishment. The administrations of Harding, Coolidge, and Hoover had been viewed as part of the establishment, closely tied to the business and financial leadership of the country. In the 1930s, however, the Roosevelt administration was considered antiestablishment, and Mencken's attacks on the New Deal sounded like a defense of the establishment. Thus, Mencken was no longer the darling of antiestablishment college sophomores, while members of the establishment found it difficult to take to their bosoms a man who had for years ridiculed them, even though they agreed with his attacks on the New Deal.[48]

The *American Mercury* opened its pages to other prominent literary critics of the New Deal and the new direction of liberalism. Albert Jay Nock, for example, wrote of 1930s liberals: "When a Liberal steams up on his emotions, they take complete charge of him. His intelligence goes on a sit-down strike; he cannot think; and therefore he runs to an incorrigibly superficial view of things, even of the thing which has riled him."[49] And author and playwright Channing Pollock wrote of the American scene after five years of the New Deal that in his 58 years he had never seen people "so universally disturbed and depressed." His travels to 123 cities and towns had brought him into contact with people from all walks of life, and he had found "practically every responsible inhabitant worried to death."

The average man who . . . up to now has been neither out-at-elbow nor down-at-heel, finds himself in a wallowing boat, without faith in the reliability of the steersman, the integrity of the crew, or the ability of the passengers to do anything about it. Five years of Planned Security have brought the greatest feeling of insecurity this commonwealth has ever known.[50]

WRITING AND READING

By the end of the 1930s the *Reader's Digest* was the most widely circulated magazine in America, perhaps because during the depression years most families could not subscribe to, or buy, all of the magazines they were accustomed to reading, and found it easier and cheaper to survey the "cream" of the other magazines as printed in the *Digest*. The depression took its toll of leading magazines like *Outlook, Century, North American Review* (after 124 years), and *Scribner's*.

Generations of college literature instructors have made the names of the proletarian, antibusiness writers of the 1930s well known, and have frequently given the impression that business was without its defenders among any literary figures other than the writers for pulp magazines. Yet, as Emily Watts has pointed out, business did have its defenders in the literary world, and those defenders grew more numerous as the 1930s went on. Curiously enough, the proletarian writers were for the most part male, while women were more likely to be found defending capitalism and businessmen. Gertrude Stein, for example, described by Watts as "undoubtedly one of our most respected writers" in the 1930s, launched a defense of capitalism in a series of five articles for *The Saturday Evening Post* in 1936. For Stein, individual freedom was intertwined with capitalism.[51]

Other literary figures altered earlier radical views after personal exposure to the vaunted collectivist "experiment" in the Soviet Union.

E. E. Cummings, for example, published in 1933 his diary (*Eimi*) of a five-week stay in the USSR. Watts writes: "What Cummings discovered in Russia stunned him from his communist sympathies: hypocrisy, the subordination of art to the state, an antiquated technology, a 'world of Was,' a land of 'people-less people,' 'a new realm whose inhabitants are made of each other,' 'a joyless experiment in force and fear.'" Gradually Cummings moved away from his earlier hopes for communism, and by 1938, he had "begun to associate economic liberty with artistic and personal liberty."[52]

"The most fully developed favorable depictions of capitalists in works by Americans in the 1930s," Watts points out, "appeared in the writings of two American women, Edna St. Vincent Millay and Ayn Rand." Millay's *Conversation at Midnight*, published in 1937, depicted its businessman character favorably by comparison with its communist. But it was Ayn Rand who, in Watts' words, "created a new American hero, the entrepreneur, a kind of old-fashioned con man and Yankee Peddler, though not viewed as a destructive person," beginning with her successful play *Night of January 16th*, which ran on Broadway in 1935, even though the full development of her hero would not be completed until after World War II.[53]

One of the most popular genres of 1930s fiction was that of the so-called tough-guy writers, whose characters and themes were similar to those popular in the movies, radio, and even comics during the depression years. Representative writers of this genre were Raymond Chandler (*The Big Sleep* and *Farewell, My Lovely*), Dashiell Hammett (*The Maltese Falcon* and *The Thin Man*), James Cain (*The Postman Always Rings Twice* and *Double Indemnity*), and Horace McCoy (*They Shoot Horses, Don't They?*). "An unusually tough era," David Madden wrote, "turns out the hard-boiled hero." The depression had caused a violent reaction in men who "lay down in the great American dream-bed of the Twenties only to wake up screaming in the nightmare of the Thirties."

In a society in which human events daily, on all levels, contradict the preachments of institutions, the tough guy is strategically placed to perceive lies and hypocrisy—he cannot live with or by them *now* as he might have under more congenial circumstances. He plays society's games—to win. In his actions more crucially than in his attitudes, he takes revenge on the forces that shaped him; however, they usually defeat him.

The style of the tough-guy writers, Madden noted, was "as terse and idiomatic as the news headlines, radio bulletins, and newsreels which reported the events of the Thirties." The characters spoke "the language of the streets, the pool rooms, the union halls, the bull pens, the factories, the hobo jungles."[54]

But, as Madden also notes, "tough-guy" literature was not the only writing in the 1930s. "During the years in which the tough novels appeared, novels reliving the romantic, historical past became a million-dollar industry. *Gone With the Wind*; Edna Ferber's *Cimarron*; Kenneth Roberts' and Walter Edmonds' novels; and Hervey Allen's *Anthony Adverse*—in a present of victims, the heroes of the past.'' Many novels, such as Louis Bromfield's *The Rains Came*, dealt with exotic, foreign worlds. Pearl Buck's *The Good Earth* offered the consoling message that others were worse off than Americans and had been for centuries. Erskine Caldwell's *Tobacco Road* was a reminder that some Americans were always in a depression. From all directions and times authors sought escapist themes to meet the needs of the readers of the 1930s.[55]

The books that had the greatest selling qualities, though, were the historical novels, and the American Civil War was for some reason especially popular. The 1930s also saw a considerable relaxation of the censorship that had still prevailed even during the roaring twenties. In January of 1934, for example, a court order made it possible, finally, for James Joyce's *Ulysses* to be sold legally in the United States.[56]

The Saturday Evening Post and *Collier's* were the mainstays of the popular magazines in the 1930s, providing in their short stories and serials the same type of escapism from depression realities that was being served up at neighborhood movie theaters and over the radio. Where fiction was concerned, in fact, it was the magazines, primarily, that showed the least influence of the depression. As in the 1920s, the fiction of magazine writers like Clarence Buddington Kelland continued to emphasize rags-to-riches stories, country club romances, and other such themes. Charles Hearn writes:

As popular writers tell and retell the old rags-to-riches story in the pages of magazines, which also have accounts of coal miners starving in Pennsylvania or ruined businessmen committing suicide, one gets the impression that the dream of success has become a fantasy, a fairy-tale escape mechanism, a secular ritual serving as a shield against hopelessness. . . . Understandably, this impulse to escape reality was strongest in the Depression years. Readers for whom the five-cent purchase price of [a magazine] was a sacrifice did not want to be reminded too often of the unpleasant reality of unemployment, hunger, and shattered dreams. They preferred light reading that would take them momentarily out of reality.[57]

And magazine advertisements similarly contributed to the illusion of another world outside that was far different from the unpleasant real one.

Declining book sales because of the depression, combined with the competition from the magazine world, led some publishers to turn to cheaper editions of classics and other popular books that could be sold through newsstands, drug and cigar stores, and other more accessible locations than merely bookstores. Pocket Books was launched in 1939, with its paperback editions of classics and best sellers marketed for 25 cents. Book clubs were also popular during the 1930s, with the original Book-of-the-Month Club and Literary Guild joined by new special-interest clubs. By their choice of *Reader's Digest* for magazine reading, and their membership in book clubs, many Americans were reading essentially the same things in the 1930s, perhaps because it made them more comfortable in knowing they were part of a "mainstream," or perhaps because it gave them a medium for conversation with others.

The 1930s also saw Americans receiving three Nobel Prizes for Literature. Sinclair Lewis received the first ever awarded to an American in 1930, and he was followed by dramatist Eugene O'Neill in 1936, and Pearl Buck in 1938. Poetry, too, showed a vitality in the 1930s that had been absent for decades and has not been seen since, in such popular works as those of Stephen Vincent Benet, Edna St. Vincent Millay, and Carl Sandburg. The latter also produced the moving four-volume biography of Abraham Lincoln.

CHAPTER FOUR

Newspapers and Radio

NEWS IN THE 1930s

Newspapers, although challenged by radio, remained the principal source of news and comment on the news, as well as a primary medium of entertainment for the family. Many newspapers contained serialized fiction, even more printed helpful hints for the depression-era housewife, including low-cost recipes (See Chapter Eight). No radio news broadcasts could deal with news in the same breadth and depth as newspapers, nor could radio offer the photographic coverage of newspapers. And even the most avid radio listeners were dependent on the newspapers for the daily broadcast schedules.

Even more than would normally be the case—except perhaps during wartime—the news from Washington was the principal running story during the 1930s. President Hoover's efforts to halt the economic downturn, the stalemate between the White House and Congress during Hoover's final years, the Bonus Marcher episode of the summer of 1932, the nominating conventions of the two parties that year and the presidential campaign and election that followed, and the banking crisis of early 1933—all were major news in the early 1930s. The arrival of Roosevelt in the White House and the beginnings of the New Deal focused even more newspaper and public attention on the often-bewildering array of actions and pronouncements that were emanating from Washington.

Crime, however, continued to capture a large share of the front pages, just as in the 1920s. Undoubtedly the most sensational story of the decade was the kidnapping and murder of the child of one of the heroes of the 1920s, Charles Lindbergh. The story of the crime, the hunt for the murderer, and then the trial continued to be front-page features from 1932 until the execution of Bruno Hauptmann in 1936. Gangster killings continued, as in the 1920s, to be front-page features, as was the trial and imprisonent of one of the leading gangsters of them all, Al Capone. Second only to crime coverage was newspaper interest in the Dionne quintuplets, who were born in 1934. The dramatic events that were occurring overseas in the 1930s likewise forced newspapers to give greater attention to foreign news and U.S. diplomacy than in the previous decade.[1]

THE NEWSPAPERS AND POLITICS

The conflict over the new antibusiness "liberalism" in general and New Deal policies in particular was especially joined in the newspapers, which were, themselves, businesses and therefore affected in important ways by the new direction of American politics. Thus, newspapers, as businesses, could be expected to share in the general business opposition to government policies viewed as hostile to business and to the capitalist system. But newspapers also have a special function in a free society that gives them peculiar responsibilities. Newspapers rightly regard themselves as tribunes of the people, defenders of the public against perceived threats to their liberties and well-being. During a period when both the opposition party and the Congress seemed unwilling or unable to meet their responsibilities as checks on the executive branch, this critical function of the press was especially important. Thus, the editorial pages of many major newspapers submitted the programs and policies of the New Deal to the kind of critical analysis that was lacking in Congress and, after a brief "honeymoon" period, many leading newspapers began to oppose Roosevelt's policies even if not always the president himself, and the number of press opponents of the New Deal grew as the 1930s went on. This, in turn, stimulated attacks on the press from the Roosevelt administration and its allies among collectivist "liberals."

The press, being capitalist, thus found itself caught in the crossfire of the class warfare that had been fomented by the Roosevelt administration since March 1933, and such attacks did not help the prestige of the press in the eyes of the public.[2] John Cowles, a midwestern newspaper publisher, wrote in 1938:

Probably, when the collectivist ideas that have temporarily seized the minds of our otherwise enlightened liberals begin to lose their hypnotic charms, attacks on the press will diminish. Newspaper publishing will then gradually regain some of its former prestige, and public confidence in newspapers will slowly return.[3]

The ability of publishers and editors to influence public opinion against the Roosevelt administration through the editorial page was largely negated, moreover, by the content of the front and other pages of their newspapers. From early in his administration, Roosevelt set out to win the support of the reporters in the White House press corps, and he succeeded to a remarkable degree. Thus, while the editorial page of a newspaper might lambaste Roosevelt or his policies, its criticism was lost in a sea of favorable news stories about the president and his administration. Roosevelt was also a master at publicizing himself through frequent trips, public appearances, speeches, and other devices, and he encouraged the same type of activity by others in his personal and official family. The president of the United States was indisputably news, and by his continual activities Roosevelt kept himself and his policies on the front pages.

COLUMNISTS

One phenomenon of the depression, especially of the New Deal years, was the growing popularity of syndicated columnists, as shown by both the increase in their number and by the growing list of newspapers that printed their columns. In a period of economic turmoil, people looked to Washington for news, and as the news became more and more complicated they also sought explanations of what it all meant. It was a period when, one reporter noted, the news in Washington went from 90 percent political and 10 percent economic, to 90 percent economic and 10 percent political. Many newsmen were as unprepared for this new emphasis on economics as were their readers, and were hard-pressed to understand it and to describe it in their columns.[4] Columnist Arthur Krock wrote that "in an era of conflicting, shifting and forming policies," the "occupation of a sand-hog is safe and tame in comparison with the perils that beset the New Deal interpreter."[5]

Columnists also tended to rely less on the official version of the news, frequently shunned White House press conferences, had acquired the cynicism of age and experience, and were thus less susceptible to a pro-New Deal bias than those who were younger and daily exposed to the Rooseveltian charm. Their columns, therefore, were valued by editors, and many readers, for their independence of the "official" line.[6]

In this "Golden Age" of newspaper columnists, some 150–200 syndicated Washington columns appeared between 1930 and 1934, most of which expired "after a brief but gaudy existence." The drama in Washington, especially with the arrival of the New Deal, focused new attention on the personalities and events in that city, causing it to rival Broadway and Hollywood as an attraction for readers of newspapers. Some political columnists were only slightly less sensational than the Broadway and Hollywood "snoops" in the gossip they reported from Washington.[7]

From the pack of syndicated columnists who attained popularity in the early 1930s, five emerged as primarily purveyors of comment rather than reporters of news: Frank Kent, David Lawrence, Walter Lippmann, Mark Sullivan, and Arthur Krock. Other syndicated political columnists, like Paul Mallon, Ray Tucker, and the duo of Drew Pearson and Robert Allen, mixed commentary with "inside" news.[8]

The five principal columnists were all veteran newsmen by 1933. The acknowledged "dean" of the columnists, however, was Walter Lippmann, of the New York *Herald-Tribune*. Frederick Lewis Allen wrote of Lippmann that "he seemed to be able to reduce a senseless sequence of events to sense; he brought first aid to men and women groping in the dark for opinions."[9]

Roosevelt's general affection for newspapermen did not extend to columnists.[10] Columnist Raymond Clapper noted that Roosevelt liked straight news reporters, but "his hair shirts in the business are the commentators, the second-guessers, the men who attempt to explain what the news means, to point out the holes in it, who tell how the magician does his tricks." Clapper wrote that Roosevelt considered this "branch of the tribe" to be "impertinent, overcurious, sometimes impudent children whose parents are not strict enough with them." The president had disliked them during his gubernatorial days in Albany, and his dislike for them was "even more pronounced" now that he was in the White House. It was easy to understand why Roosevelt "should have a feeling of frustration about these men," Clapper wrote. "Because the commentators are free to explain and interpret, he can not control their output as he can with reporters restricted to reproducing only the master's voice."[11]

Beginning with Sullivan, Kent, and Krock, the leading columnists began even in 1933 to express serious misgivings about the New Deal policies and programs, and they were joined as the 1930s went on by Lippmann and others. Yet even when their columns were joined in opposition with the editorial pages, the newspapers seemed unable to influence public sentiment away from Roosevelt, personally, even when the president also became less attractive to the Washington press corps in the second half of the 1930s. While the more literate of newspaper readers might have been influenced by the arguments of columnists like Sullivan and Lippmann, the "escapist" mood of most Americans during the decade probably led them to avoid such attempts to deal with the grim realities of those years. Whatever the reason, Roosevelt was able to win reelection handily in 1936 and 1940, despite the opposition of a majority of the nation's newspapers.

PUBLIC OPINION POLLS AND NEWS PHOTOS

A new feature of American journalism in the 1930s was the beginnings of scientific public opinion polling. Attempts to poll public opinion were not new, but until the arrival of Dr. George Gallup's poll in the 1930s, such samplings had been largely haphazard even when their results were accurate. The polls of *Literary Digest* magazine are best remembered and were remarkably accurate in the 1920s and early 1930s. The gross inaccuracy of its poll in predicting a Landon victory over Roosevelt in 1936, however, brought about the demise of both the poll and the magazine.

That the *Literary Digest* Poll had been correct for a time, however, was shown by Gallup Polls early in the 1936 campaign, which also found Landon ahead of Roosevelt in electoral votes, although trailing in popular votes. Even a poll for the Democratic National Committee showed Landon beating Roosevelt early in the year. If there was any doubt that the American people were uncomfortable with the New Deal, it should have been answered by yet another Gallup Poll, released in August 1936, which found an amazing 45 percent of Americans polled answering "yes" to the question: "Do you believe the acts and policies of the Roosevelt administration may lead to dictatorship?" Probably no president in American history had aroused such concern over the possibility of dictatorship in this country. Indeed, it is difficult to imagine the question being asked by a responsible pollster during the administration of any other president but Roosevelt.

Gradually, as the campaign progressed through the summer months and into the fall, Roosevelt overtook Landon in the Gallup Polls. The initial enthusiasm for Landon abated as the Kansan revealed himself as a lackluster campaigner unwilling or unable to offer alternatives to the New Deal, but apparently intent, instead, on trying to outbid Roosevelt for the support of various interest groups, especially farmers. Meanwhile, within the Roosevelt administration all stops had been pulled out to make sure that government funds would obtain the maximum number of votes on election day. With a Gallup Poll showing that 75.1 percent of the relief vote was for Roosevelt and only 17.5 percent for Landon, it was obviously politic to inflate, rather than deflate, the relief rolls in an election year.

As election day approached it became clear that misgivings about Roosevelt did not automatically mean support for Landon. In addition, as Mark Sullivan pointed out in mid-October, memories of the stalemate between a Republican president and a Democratic Congress were still vivid from the final two years of Hoover's administration, so that many Democrats with misgivings about Roosevelt were likely not to vote for Landon, lest his election create the same sort of stalemate now. Despite prominent defections from the Democratic camp, including the 1924 and 1928 presidential candidates of the party, John W. Davis and Al Smith, the Gallup Poll showed Roosevelt increasing his lead over Landon in mid-October, with 390 electoral votes against 141 for Landon. Gallup now foresaw a possible "landslide in the Electoral College if the present trend continues unaltered." The final Gallup Poll, released in the newspapers on November 1st, found only three states sure for Landon—Maine, Vermont and New Hampshire—with Roosevelt guaranteed at least 315 electoral votes, more than enough to win. The only weakness in the poll was Gallup's failure to poll right up until the eve of the election to gauge last-minute shifts. Had he done so, Gallup might well have predicted the shift of New Hampshire to FDR, leaving Landon only two states.

Given the results of the early Gallup (and Democratic) Polls, it seems clear that the combination of Landon's inept campaign and massive New Deal election-year spending offers a better explanation for the trend in the polls. Had Roosevelt been as popular as historians later claimed, it is doubtful it he would have trailed in the early Gallup or Democratic National Committee polls.[12]

New developments in newsgathering contributed to the success of the newspapers in the 1930s. The Associated Press inaugurated wirephoto services on January 1, 1935, with 24 stations initially serving 39 newspapers.[13] Its use quickly spread to other newspapers and brought competitors into the field, notably Hearst, the New York *Times* (Wired Photos), and Scripps-Howard (NEA-Acme Telephoto), all in the 1930s. As a result, newspaper readers found more photographs in their newspapers, with the metropolitan dailies increasing their photo content by about two-thirds, reaching 38 percent of an issue by 1938.[14] As might be expected, the growing use of photographs led to the rise of specialized news photographers who now began to accompany reporters in covering stories.

THE COMPETITION FROM NEWSMAGAZINES

The 1930s also saw the growing popularity and proliferation of newsmagazines. Henry Luce's *Time* magazine predated the 1930s (1923), but it was now joined by what Frederick Lewis Allen called "its younger sister," *Fortune*, and by *Life* (1936), which satisfied the public's desire for dramatic photojournalism in the pre-television era and which was also, in part at least, a product of the camera craze of the 1930s. *Today*, founded by ex-New Dealer Raymond Moley and Vincent Astor, began as a new journal generally supportive of the New Deal, but it became more critical as Moley and Astor grew disenchanted with Roosevelt. *Newsweek* likewise was founded in 1933 by an Englishman, Thomas J. C. Martyn, who had worked for *Time*. Vincent Astor became its principal stockholder in 1937 and merged it with *Today*, after which *Newsweek* featured Moley's weekly editorials generally critical of the New Deal. *United States News* (now *U.S. News and World Report*) also began in 1933 as a weekly newsmagazine in newspaper format, founded and edited by David Lawrence, who was also a leading syndicated columnist. Lawrence, too, in his syndicated columns and his editorials in *United States News*, grew increasingly critical of the New Deal despite a long acquaintance with Roosevelt that dated back to World War I.

The competition for newspapers posed by the rise of the newsmagazines led some newspapers to begin printing "news-in-review" sections on Sundays, beginning with the Cincinnati *Enquirer* in 1930. The New York *Times* began its "News of the Week in Review" section in 1935, which not only summarized the news but also contained special articles by Washington and foreign correspondents. The New York *Herald-Tribune* offered its "History in the Making" section, and other similar weekly news summaries were offered by one or two leading newspapers in almost every part of the country by the end of the 1930s.[15]

FOR THE LOVELORN

Almost every newspaper in America also pandered to the cravings that made the true confessions magazines so popular in the 1930s through their "advice to the lovelorn" columns. Dorothy Dix was the most popular in the 1930s and her column was syndicated daily in a newspaper in almost every city or town. Beatrice Fairfax, a trade name behind which a succession of writers labored, was taken up by most of their competitors, while smaller newspapers had their own columns. Readers could eavesdrop while others spilled out their domestic and romantic problems in ink. Some newspapers even sponsored "clubs" through which they acted as the medium for the development of potential romances. In the competition with radio and magazines for circulation in the 1930s, the newspapers tried to meet as many reader needs as possible.

STANDARDIZATION AND THE TABLOIDS

One result of the growth of syndication, the use of news services like the Associated Press and United Press, the introduction of wirephotos, and other aspects of journalism in the 1930s was a trend toward standardization in newspapers all across the country. It was but one aspect of an increasing standardization of American life under the impact of the technological advances of the 1920s and 1930s—the automobile, radio, the movies, and others. Newspapers, Robert Benchley complained, had achieved a "universal sameness" by the early 1930s. Except for a very few exceptional newspapers like the New York *Times*, the Baltimore *Sun*, and the Kansas City *Star*, newspapers in America were so undistinguishable, one from the other, that a traveler to another city might confuse its newspaper for that of his hometown except for the difference in local news. So dependent had some newspapers become on the wire services for their news stories that they were operating with only one or two reporters on their payrolls.[16]

An unsavory exception to this standardization was the tabloid newspapers of the large cities, which were immensely popular during the 1930s. Tabloid newspapers were a conspicuous area of success in journalism during the 1930s, with their number growing from a dozen in 1930 to 35 dailies and one Sunday edition by 1936. Tabloids like the New York *Daily News* were, however, interested mainly in those news stories that could be sensationalized, and their standards of veracity and ethics were considered so low by their critics that they scarcely deserved to be described as newspapers at all in the 1930s. Robert Benchley categorized them as "daily magazines, and very low-class magazines at that." As they tended to be filled with photographs illustrating whatever sensational stories they were featuring, the tabloids were convenient for those newspaper "readers" who wanted to look rather than read, while their smaller size made them convenient for commuters on trains and subways. Thanks to the tabloids, Benchley wrote, "the public is now supplied with its full quota of murders, divorces, rapes, and gossip without having to take the trouble of looking through columns of international or civic news to find it."[17] That the public desired such fare is clear, however, from a 1935 New York City survey, which showed that two-thirds of the city's youths read the tabloids, while nearly one-fifth read no other kind of newspaper.[18]

THE RISE OF RADIO

Newspapers found their principal competition in radio, which grew to maturity during the decade of the 1930s, developing into a well-rounded source of information and entertainment for the entire family. This medium, which had scarcely existed as recently as 1920, transformed American life to a degree and with a rapidity that was unprecedented except perhaps in the case of the automobile. By the 1930s, one study noted, radio had transformed all of America "into a vast auditorium, into all corners of which a single voice can carry with dramatic ease and clarity." But, the same study warned, radio offered potential for both good and evil. It was "terrifying because of the possibilities it opens for the accomplishment of selfish ends."[19]

The 1930s saw considerable improvement in radio programming, at least in part forced by a loss of listeners during the early years of the depression when studies showed a decline in the number of radios owned. Among Iowa farmers, for example, ownership of radios declined by nearly 30 percent during 1932, with only one in three farms owning a radio in 1933 as compared to nearly one-half in 1931.[20] Other studies showed a decline of 25 percent in listeners during the first two years of depression.[21] Clearly, either the effects of the depression were cutting into radio listenership, or radio was losing popularity.

By early 1933, however, the Child Study Association of America was already reporting that children had become constant radio listeners and that parents were disturbed over the influence that radio was exerting over young listeners.[22] Maxine Davis found radio second only to the movies as the "opiate" of youth. "They sit at home and get all the excitement of a football game—at third hand," she wrote. "They shave to the latest sentimental song. They giggle at the jokes of comedians, good or bad. They find their laughter by a twist of a dial." The whole generation was "living passively, vicariously," "finding its fun in unreality."[23]

When the Lynds returned to Middletown in 1935, they found "everywhere the blare of radios was more pervasive than in 1925." And when the Chamber of Commerce solicited suggestions from Middletonians on how the city might be improved, one suggestion was to "abolish noisy radios up and down the streets."[24] Clearly the use of radios had become so pervasive that the cumulative noise was intruding beyond the homes.

In 1937, CBS reported that ownership of radios, numbers of listeners, and hours of average listening time had grown dramatically in the past year. Its study showed that 24.5 million Americans owned radios and were buying them at the rate of 28 per minute. Over 1.6 million families had joined the radio audience during 1936 and listening time was up from 4.1 hours per day in 1935 to a little more than 5 hours per day in 1936. Some 4 million families owned more than one radio, and 4.5 million had radios in their automobiles. The higher the family's income the more likely they were to own a radio, but the lower the income the more likely the family was to actually listen to it. CBS concluded its study with the observation that Americans were devoting 95.5 million family hours per day to radio listening, "enough, if set end to end to extend back in time to 8,942 B.C."[25] In 1938, Louis Reid estimated the weekly output of words by a single radio station at 800,000, which meant that the 600-odd stations in the nation were flooding the country with a total of nearly 500 million words in a single week.[26]

PROGRAMMING

Daytime programming was designed for housewives laboring in their homes. At 4:30 p.m. the focus switched to the children returning home from school. Children's shows frequently offered premiums like "official" rings, secret decoders, badges, whistles, membership kits, and the like to those listeners who would mail in the required number of boxtops and perhaps a dime or quarter. At suppertime, then as now, the focus was on the newscast, after which during "prime time," children would gather with parents to escape into the world of music, comedy, drama, game shows, or crime—unless the latter were deemed too violent for the children.

It is tempting to conclude that listenership increased because of improved programming, as some historians of radio assert. It could as easily have occurred because more families could afford radios after 1933, or because more of them found as the depression went on that they could afford no other entertainment than evenings in front of the radio. Certainly one reason for the boom was the declining price of radio sets. Before the 1930s the average set was bulky and expensive. Manufacturers were quick to recognize that consumers could spend less money now on nonessentials like radios, and they responded by producing cheaper sets. The trend in sales of radio sets between 1930 and 1933 was away from costly console models and toward low-priced table models.[27] "Simultaneously," Deems Taylor wrote, "as people found themselves with no spending money for theatres, night clubs, and vaudeville, they stayed home, perforce, and bought those portable sets in order to have something to listen to during the lean winter evenings."[28] The result was that by 1935 the Lynds found not only more radios, but more time being spent listening to each one.[29]

One obvious reason for acquiring at least one of the cheaper new sets was to keep abreast of what was happening in Washington. With the inauguration of Franklin Delano Roosevelt as president of the United States in March 1933, the radio began immediately to be used by the new president and members of his administration to explain the new policies and programs. Beginning with Roosevelt's "fireside chat" on the banking crisis, Americans found that their president was a compelling radio personality in his own right (ranked in a *Fortune* magazine poll of 1938 as America's number 11 radio personality[30]), and that the Roosevelt administration regarded radio as the front line in their attempts to communicate directly with the public. Families without radios would have to rely, instead, on their friends and neighbors for the latest news on New Deal developments—not a pleasing prospect.

The result, as Alice Marquis has pointed out, was that citizens could now gather in front of the radio and hear the voices and proposals of their politicians to a degree that had not been possible since the days of the ancient Greek polis. At the same time, the radio was responsible for much of the standardization of speech, manners, and tastes from one end of the country to the other that was so decried by those who appreciated America's diversity.[31]

Yet there is no doubt that the quality of radio programming did begin to improve in the early 1930s and that it continued to improve and to diversify as the decade went on. Radio began as a musical medium and through the 1920s it remained principally a source of music and discussion. Music remained important in the 1930s, but new types of programs were introduced early in the decade and attained rapid popularity.

COMEDY AND VARIETY SHOWS

The "Amos 'n' Andy" comedy show, which began airing in 1929, was the most popular radio program during the early 1930s, with perhaps 40 million listeners. Arthur Wertheim reports that during the 15-minute radio program, telephone use declined and department stores were forced to pipe in the six-times-a-week broadcasts to keep shoppers from going home. Movie theaters similarly installed loudspeakers in their lobbies and on their stages, and stopped their films so that theater patrons would not miss the latest adventures on the show. The alternative was to lose patrons to the radio. Some businesses closed early to allow their workers to listen.[32] Bruce Bliven reported that many people refused "to answer the telephone during the sacred quarter of an hour, and one man even inserted an advertisement in a newspaper asking his friends not to bother him while the broadcast is in progress."[33]

"Amos 'n' Andy," one historian writes, "captured the fancy of the nation and turned a popular medium into a mass medium." The show spawned toys, candy bars, a comic strip, and phonograph records.[34] More importantly, it spawned other comedy broadcasts, as the appeal of comedy for depression-ridden Americans became obvious as a result of their popularity.

During the 1930s radio mirrored most of the developments that were taking place in the other entertainment media, providing aurally what Americans during the depression were absorbing visually from the comic strips, popular literature, and films, while at the same time moving the best of vaudeville from the stage to the radio microphone. Like the other media, the emphasis of radio broadcasting was on escape from the reality of the depression.

Radio and the movies killed vaudeville, but also provided new and greater opportunities for the best comedians from that entertainment field. In the early 1930s, radio featured such ex-vaudevillians as Ed Wynn, George Burns and Gracie Allen, Jack Benny, George Jessel, and Fred Allen in popular comedy shows. The first vaudeville veteran to attain success in radio was Eddie Cantor, who had also attained celebrity status in the movies and in music. The Eddie Cantor show ("The Chase and Sanborn Hour"), which first aired in the fall of 1931, quickly became one of the most popular programs on radio. Unlike the situation comedy of "Amos 'n' Andy," the inspiration for the Cantor show was almost entirely vaudeville—with live audiences, fast patter, and good supporting acts. Previous to Cantor, radio broadcasts had been done without spectators, or with the spectators sealed from the studio by glass so that their noise would not go out over the air.[35]

The success of Cantor led the networks to bring in other ex-vaudevillians and the early 1930s saw radio dominated by the comedians. One of the most popular for a time was Ed Wynn, who debuted as "The Fire Chief" in April 1932 and attained a rating of 44.8 by 1933, which meant that nearly one-half of the surveyed homes were listening to his program. Thereafter his ratings steadily declined, however, and the program went off the air in 1935.[36] Meanwhile, other ex-vaudevillians were developing new nonvaudevillian formats for comedy broadcasts—the most notable and successful of whom was Jack Benny. From his debut on network radio in 1932, Benny began to create the tightwad image that would be his trademark during 21 years of success on the radio, followed by television stardom. Another situation comedy that attained great popularity during the 1930s was "Fibber McGee and Molly," with their supporting cast of daffy characters in the town of Wistful Vista.

Will Rogers began his own radio program in 1930 and until he died in an airplane crash five years later he was, one historian observes, "the court jester and critical wit of the nation."[37] As both comedian and commentator, Rogers did not fit the mold of most radio programming in the 1930s, which was concerned chiefly with providing escape and diversion from the depression. Instead, Rogers confronted the depression head on and reflected in his broadcasts the same bewilderment that his fellow Americans felt over their predicament and the inability of government and business leaders to produce recovery.

Typical of Rogers' realism was his rejection of flowers as an appropriate Mother's Day gift during the depression, since flowers couldn't be eaten. Instead, Rogers recommended more practical gifts during the depression— like meat.[38] Generally Rogers backed Roosevelt in his efforts to improve the economy, encouraging businesses to enroll under the National Recovery Administration in 1933, for example. But he was as bewildered as most Americans over the apparent reversal of values that was taking place under the New Deal, observing, for example: "We're living in a peculiar time. You get more for not working than you will for working, and more for not raising a hog than raising it."[39]

DRAMA FOR ALL AGES

From the comic strips came such popular characters as Dick Tracy, Little Orphan Annie, Buck Rogers, and Flash Gordon with their own programs on Saturday mornings and in after-school hours. Other action and adventure programs were also designed specifically for children, such as "Jack Armstrong, The All American Boy," and "Jungle Jim." As was the case with comic strips, the programs designed for children—and others listened to by children—were often filled with violence. This drew increasing criticism through the 1930s, and eventually resulted in the networks adopting policy codes designed to reduce the level of violence on programs listened to by children.[40]

The popularity of crime as a subject of movies and comic strips was mirrored on radio in such programs of the 1930s as "Gangbusters," "Sherlock Holmes," "The Shadow," "Mr. Keen, Tracer of Lost Persons," and "The Green Hornet," many of which were also listened to by children although aired during adult listening hours. Like gangster movies, crime programs were appealing to radio executives because they could be made cheaply, and although they seldom ranked high in the ratings, they "delivered more listeners per dollar than did the comedy and variety series."[41]

J. Fred MacDonald has identified two major types of detective shows in the 1930s: the "realistic detectives" and the "glamorous detectives." In the former, the listening audience was given clues and expected to solve the crime in such programs as "Sherlock Homes," "Gangbusters," and "Mr. District Attorney." In the latter, the character of the hero was at least as important as the story lines. Typical of this type were Lamont Cranston in his role as "The Shadow," "The Green Hornet," and "Mr. Keen, Tracer of Lost Persons."[42]

Daytime radio, particularly the soap operas, also offered an opportunity for Americans to escape the depression and enter a world of romance and adventure in the 1930s. The success of such evening programs as "Amos 'n' Andy" suggested that serialized stories might work equally well during the daytime. Certainly more Americans were at home with time on their hands during the depression than in normal times, and they were ready for radio programming that would furnish escape and amusement during the daytime hours. The success of soap operas in filling these needs can be seen in their growth from 3 in 1931 to 10 in 1934, 31 in 1936, and 61 by 1939. An architect of many of the most successful soaps of the 1930s found his inspiration in the successful serial fiction in newspapers and magazines. "It occurred to me," he said, "that what people were reading might appeal to them in the form of radio dramas."[43]

This radio equivalent of the escapism in popular newspaper and magazine fiction took the form of such programs as "Mrs. Wiggs of the Cabbage Patch," "Painted Dreams," "Today's Children," "Ma Perkins," "The Romance of Helen Trent," "Just Plain Bill," "Backstage Wife," "Our Gal Sunday," "Lorenzo Jones," "Stella Dallas," and "Young Widder Brown," many of which endured until well into the 1950s.[44] In these radio dramas women were frequently the featured characters, as befitted programs aired principally to female audiences.

RADIO NEWS

Radio also joined, and began to compete with, the newspapers in gathering and broadcasting news in the 1930s. Before 1933 newspapers had provided news material free of charge to radio stations for their own news broadcasts, but in 1932 the newspapers began to resent the growing competition that the radio networks were furnishing them. In 1933 the Associated Press (AP) voted to provide no more news to networks, and soon the United Press (UP) and the International News Service (INS) adopted similar rules. News bulletins from the AP, UP, and INS would be available for a fee to some individual stations, but not to the networks. Rather than give up their news broadcasts, the networks began to gather their own news. At NBC, Lowell Thomas and Walter Winchell aired the news, while CBS was represented by H. V. Kaltenborn and Boake Carter. Attempts by the newspapers and the news services to stifle the new competition from the networks succeeded briefly in early 1934, but eventually money won out. Advertiser interest in sponsoring radio news broadcasts eventually caused UP and INS to break with AP and to begin making their news available for sponsored broadcasts, and AP was forced to follow suit.[45]

By 1939 a Roper Poll showed that more than 25 percent of the population relied principally on radio as its source of news. Many of the radio newscasters of the 1930s were former newspaper columnists who had abandoned the printed page for the airwaves, or who worked in both media. Floyd Gibbons, William L. Shirer, Edwin C. Hill, Raymond Gram Swing, and H. R. Baukage were some who came to radio from the newspapers, while Walter Winchell, Dorothy Thompson, Drew Pearson, and Boake Carter worked in both media.[46]

Radio paralleled the newspapers in the 1930s by developing its own news commentators, the number growing from a half-dozen at the beginning of the 1930s to nearly 20 by the end of the decade. Radio stations were, however, subject to licensing by the federal government and radio commentators therefore lacked the freedom enjoyed by their newspaper counterparts to be critical of Roosevelt and his policies. Their comments, Irving Fang has observed, were "often rather mild, a dash of catsup compared to the tabasco sauce served up in the newspapers." One exception was Boake Carter, who during the mid-1930s was, according to Fang, "the most popular radio news commentator in the United States and a pain in the neck to the New Deal." From 1936 to 1938 Carter ranked with Lowell Thomas of NBC at the top of the ratings, and in the latter year, when he was heard by an estimated 5–10 million listeners over 85 stations, he was voted the most popular radio commentator by readers of *Radio Guide*. In 1937 he also began to write a newspaper column for the Philadelphia *Ledger* syndicate, that by 1938 was carried by 52 newspapers with a readership estimated at 7 million. This meant that his column had wider circulation than those of such well-known journalists as Raymond Clapper, Walter Lippmann and Westbrook Pegler.[47]

While radio journalists remained for the most part a rather bland lot during the 1930s, the medium nevertheless offered a forum for opponents of the New Deal in other ways and for their own purposes. Huey Long and Father Charles Coughlin, for example, made skillful use of the airwaves to launch their own attacks and crusades. By 1935, one observer could conclude that whereas radio had in the early 1930s been "almost wholly pro-New Deal," now "the ether is disturbed nightly with waves of attack and counter-attack."[48] Thus, while the radio networks and individual stations were rarely critical of the New Deal, they did furnish a medium for New Deal opponents who offered alternative perspectives to the propaganda that was being disseminated by the Roosevelt administration.

Radio developed one distinctive approach to the news that the newspapers could not do nearly as well, if at all. This was the inauguration of panel discussions featuring experts who could explore all aspects of current debates and events. The "University of Chicago Roundtable" premiered in February 1931 and was followed by "America's Town Meeting of the Air" and by others.[49] Radio also gave Americans the opportunity to hear and evaluate political figures—both American and foreign—as had never before been possible. In this way, too, radio offered a unique contribution that the newspapers could not duplicate.

Radio also gave Americans ringside seats to the action at the nominating conventions of the Republicans and Democrats as they unfolded, and it also influenced the proceedings. In 1940 *Editor and Publisher* remarked that during the 1930s the "conventions have been staged as much for the radio as they have for the nomination of candidates, it has seemed to some observers. Business has been strung out over four or five days when it might be concluded in two, if business was the only consideration."[50]

Newspapers found radio competing with them for sports coverage, with an increasing number of sports events broadcast live during the 1930s. Louis Reid found heavyweight boxing matches drawing the largest audiences of any radio broadcasts in the late 1930s, and broadcasts of sports events in general were drawing women's attention to sports in greater numbers than ever before.[51]

FADS

While radio reflected the trends in the other entertainment media of the 1930s, it also mirrored the fads and crazes of everyday life during the depression, and the inconstancy of American popular tastes. One of the best examples of this is radio's contribution to the get-rich-quick desire of Americans during the depression. It began with the debut of "Major Bowes' Original Amateur Hour" in 1934. This show offered contestants from all over the nation a chance to compete for prizes and possible stardom, and it quickly became the top-rated program in radio, forcing the other networks to add similar shows.[52]

By 1937, however, the amateur talent shows had been eclipsed by quiz shows. Beginning with "Professor Quiz" in mid-1936, which paid $10 to the contestant most successful in answering its questions, the quiz show fad spread rapidly to all of the networks. By 1938 radio quiz shows were competing with movie bank nights and bingo, and with the nickel snatchers, for the attention of Americans through such programs as "Information Please," "The World Game," "Kay Kyser's Kollege of Musical Knowledge," "Beat the Band," "It Pays to Be Ignorant," and "Can You Top This?" The trend culminated with the appearance of "Pot O'Gold" on NBC in 1939, which offered $1,000 to anyone who picked up the telephone when called by its host, and a consolation prize of $100 to anyone not at home when called. "Movie houses," one historian wrote, "lost a considerable number of patrons during the Pot O' Gold broadcast."[53]

THEATER OVER THE AIR

Radio also competed with movie theaters by offering high-quality dramatic programming that included some of the most popular Hollywood stars in adaptations of their best films. Listeners could hear for free in the comfort of their own homes William Powell and Myrna Loy doing *The Thin Man*, or Clark Gable and Claudette Colbert in the radio version of *It Happened One Night*. Original dramas, too, were offered on a variety of programs that included the "Lux Radio Theater," "The Screen Guild Players," "Warner Academy Theater," and the "Cavalcade of America."[54]

Radio could also offer aurally at much less cost the prestige drama on which Hollywood was reluctant to gamble due to the expense of elaborate sets, extras, and other necessities for large-scale visual productions. In the second half of the 1930s, radio offered the major works of Tolstoy, Shakespeare, Hugo, Ibsen, Marlow, and others in which noted actors and actresses were featured. The cultural leadership of radio over films was further cemented by network offerings of classical music and opera. The result was that by the end of the 1930s radio was a serious competitor with newspapers as the source of news and with the film industry as a source of entertainment.[55]

RADIO'S INFLUENCE ON DAILY LIFE

The result of it all was that many lives began to be organized around the daily radio schedules. As one writer described it in the New York *Herald-Tribune Magazine*:

The lives of most of my friends seem to be governed by radio programs. In planning any social function, one must allow for the vagaries of the Charlie-McCarthophiles, the Jack-Bennyites, the Eddie-Cantorians, the Information

Pleasers, and other devotees of ethereal cults; and the East Teabone Friday Evening Bridge Club has disbanded simply because it is impossible to get a quorum any more. When I hear my host and hostess speaking in a preoccupied manner, and seem them glancing surreptitiously at the clock, I no longer feel constrained to say, "Well, I guess I'd better be running along." Instead, I say, "How about turning on the radio?" And it is gratifying to observe the eagerness with which they respond to my suggestion.[56]

Perhaps it was this preoccupation with the radio, as much as the shortage of money during the depression, that caused the decline of socializing during the 1930s.

One result of radio's hold over the American people in the 1930s was the enormous economic influence it began to exert through its commercials. Foster Dulles wrote:

A flood of orders was the invariable response when announcers told a gullible public (after the heroine had been swung over the edge of a cliff, or the swing band had emitted its last squawk) that now was the time to change the winter oil—or winter underwear—or that a special liver pill would relieve that tired feeling. Never before had entertainment become not only such a big business in itself, but also an integral part of the country's basic economic system.[57]

FM AND TELEVISION

Two major radio-related technological developments of the 1930s exerted little of the influence that they might have on popular culture because of delays in their implementation. One of these was the perfection of frequency-modulation (FM) radio broadcasting. Late in 1933, Edwin Howard Armstrong produced the first FM transmitter and receiver, and static-free radio was born. Despite this promising beginning, however, Armstrong had to wait six years before the first FM station would air. That station, the 50,000-watt W2XMN, reached full power early in 1939, and the quality of its broadcast was so clearly superior that it set off a boom in FM development until World War II began.[58]

The delay in FM development was in large part because of the commitment of RCA, Armstrong's sponsor, to the development of television as its first priority. NBC had begun experimental telecasts in 1932, and David Sarnoff, head of RCA, was obsessed with a desire to make his company the pioneer of the new technology, which he already visualized as becoming a feature in every home. Looking ahead to the New York World's Fair to be held in 1939, Sarnoff decided to make it a showcase for the new technology, the debut of scheduled commercial television broadcasts. On April 30, 1939, Franklin D. Roosevelt became the first president of the United States to appear on television when his speech opening the fair was televised. Programs were telecast to the fair daily from NBC studios, and RCA TV sets with 5- and 9-inch screens were offered for sale at prices ranging from $199.50 to $600. Television had been launched, but would have to await the end of World War II for its full development.[59] According to the Federal Communications Commission only about 1,000 television receivers had been sold to the public by late 1939, most of them in New York City.

CHAPTER FIVE

Music, Movies, and the Arts

THE INFLUENCE OF RADIO

One of the major contributions of radio in the 1930s was the popularization of music, especially the 1930s version of jazz music—what came to be known in the second half of the decade as "swing." People who were ordinarily suspicious of anything labeled "art," who might never have set foot in a concert hall even if they lived near one and could afford the price of a ticket, were now exposed to classical music and opera in their homes via radio. As Deems Taylor put it, "now, for the first time in our history, our entire people has been given access to music, regardless of financial or geographical conditions." For a time, in fact, it looked as if the availability of music on radio "might destroy all forms of public musical entertainment," since it was free at a time when few could afford the extravagance of a concert ticket.[1]

A SLOWER TEMPO

The seeds of swing had already been planted in the late 1920s by bands like those of Guy Lombardo and Rudy Vallee, who played the big-band sound that Barry Ulanov described as "country-club music"—"soft, sometimes sedate, sometimes bouncy." Lombardo's appeal, Ulanov observed, came from the band's use of its saxophones, whereas Vallee relied on a "more conventional merging of violins and saxophones, a gentle joining of related colors that soothed audiences and supplied his megaphone murmurings with a subdued background." With the onset of the depression, "American audiences wanted no part of their troubles when they sank into movie-palace horsehair [seats], nor did they want a music that deserted their narcotized retreats. America wanted the music that was played in the country clubs of its dreams, and it got it."[2]

Dancing showed the influence of the new, slower, music. The frenetic exercises of the 1920s lost ground in the early 1930s to the waltz, foxtrot, and other comparatively sedate dances. The combination of slower music and dances promoted, one historian observes, "a new innovation in America, the dancing school." Existing schools were "forced to meet the growing rush of customers," and new schools were formed to satisfy the demand.[3]

Both Lombardo and Vallee owed their success to the exposure they obtained through their radio broadcasts. Lombardo's influence on other bands began, however, after his band moved to the Hotel Roosevelt in New York City in 1930. Rudy Vallee's warm tenor voice, amplified through his trademark megaphone, will always remain an image of the 1930s. Paul Sann described the conflicts that raged in American homes between male and female members when the soft nasal tones of the Vagabond Lover's voice were coming over the airwaves. Battles ensued when the man of the house wanted the radio off or changed to another station. At least one man died in such a struggle. Vallee, says Sann, "was more than just a singer; he was an issue." His personal appearances were mob scenes; he starred in one movie in the 1930s and appeared in two Broadway shows, and his income soared to the staggering figure, during depression years, of $20,000 per week.[4]

Vallee's success as a megaphone "crooner" led other bandleaders to regard vocalists as essential adjuncts to dance bands. Quickly, two singers rose to the forefront by 1931 on rival radio networks: Bing Crosby and Russ Columbo. Crosby would go on to become "the most magnetic musical personality ever."[5] While Vallee's nasal crooning and mannerisms made him more than a little suspect among men, Crosby appealed to both sexes. The King of Groaners quickly surpassed Vallee's popularity, crooning love songs like "I Surrender, Dear" to the ladies, and cowboy songs like "Home on the Range" for the men.[6]

Crosby's preeminence was challenged late in the decade by a newcomer from Hoboken, but "Der Bingel" retained his popularity. Francis Albert Sinatra was the only winner (as part of a group called "The Hoboken Four") of the Major Bowes Amateur Hour competition to go on to stardom. He eventually joined the Harry James Band in 1939 and began his string of hits with "All or Nothing At All" in that year.

Although dance bands like Lombardo's and Vallee's were doing well in the early years of the depression, jazz had almost disappeared from the American scene, despite its continued popularity in Europe. "The mood of the 'twenties had evaporated," Marshall Stearns wrote, "and the public seemed to want only quiet, soothing dance music."[7] Yet there were exceptions to this rule, most notably the band of Duke Ellington. In the early 1930s Ellington's "hot" jazz began to be influenced by, and to exert a major influence on, the "sweet" music of the dance bands. In early February 1932 Ellington recorded the tune "It Don't Mean a Thing If It Ain't Got That Swing," and thereby "named the whole era that was to follow in three years."[8] Slightly more than a year later, prohibition was repealed, the speakeasies ended, and jazz and its musicians came more into the open.

THE AGE OF SWING

By 1935 the musical mood of Americans had clearly changed. Whether because of improved economic conditions or boredom with the sweet version of jazz offered by the country-club dance bands of Lombardo and the others, Americans were now ready for hot jazz but with the big-band sound. One jazz historian wrote: "The Depression was fading out as far as middle-class America was concerned, and a vociferous market sprang up among the college kids. They liked their music hot and their bands big. And they could pay for it."[9] They got it for the first time from the Benny Goodman orchestra, and Goodman's chief arranger Fletcher Henderson.

Goodman's band had already developed a following in the nation through its Saturday night broadcasts on the National Biscuit program over NBC. In 1935 Goodman took his band on the road, coast to coast, playing sweet music and the tour was a disaster. When they reached the Palomar Ballroom in Los Angeles in August, Goodman decided that if the band was going to flop it would do it playing the kind of music he liked. So the band launched into its swing offerings with an enthusiastic response from the audience, and the "swing era" was born.[10] Hot jazz was back, and through the big bands—both on and off radio—it was attracting larger audiences than earlier jazz musicians had ever dreamed of reaching. So influential were Goodman and the best of the other swing bands that "all but the most sickly commercial bands tightened their ensembles, offered moments of swinging section performance and even a solo or two that were jazz-infected" in order to capitalize on the popularity of swing music.[11]

"A good swing band smashing away at full speed, with the trumpeters and clarinetists rising in turn under the spotlight to embroider the theme with their several furious improvisations and the drummers going into long-drawnout rhythmical frenzies," Frederick Lewis Allen wrote, "could reduce its less inhibited auditors to sheer emotional vibration, punctuated by howls of rapture." The fever for swing music reached its climax in the winter of 1937–38, Allen observed, "when the bespectacled Mr. Goodman, playing at the Paramount and later in Boston and elsewhere, found that the boys and girls so yelled and screamed and cavorted when his band began to 'send' that a concert became a bedlam.'' A Carnival of Swing was held at Randall's Island, New York, in the spring of 1938, at which 23,000 swing fans (''jitterbugs'') cavorted enthusiastically before 25 bands for nearly six hours.[12]

Clearly, many Americans had abandoned the sedate dances of the early 1930s. Jitterbugging was the name given to the dance steps done to swing music that went under various names like ''Truckin','' the ''Shag,'' the ''Yam,'' and ''The Big Apple.'' The latter even spawned its own music. So fast did the new fads appear that dance schools like the new Arthur Murray chain were hard-pressed to keep their students *au courant*.[13]

The New York *Herald-Tribune* wondered if ''the more fanatical devotees of swing music'' were not ''just a shade on the balmy side,'' after the Randall's Island concert. The antics of young people (and some not so young), it wrote, ''resembled nothing so much as one of those waves of religious insanity which used to sweep across Europe in the Middle Ages.'' The swing culture, moreover, had created its own language—unintelligible to the uninitiated—''consisting of such odd terms as jitterbugs, alligators, ickies and so on.'' But, the *Tribune* wrote, the economic contribution of the swing culture should not be underestimated, as shown by the fact that in 1937 the production of musical instruments had exceeded that of 1935 by some 75 percent, reaching a value of nearly $34 million. The impact of swing on this increase was clear, because the sale of old-fashioned instruments like banjos and guitars was down, while those of swing instruments—pianos, clarinets (Goodman), trombones (Tommy Dorsey), drums, and others had risen. The newspaper concluded: ''Maybe car loads and the production of pig iron, the old standbys of the business prophets, don't look so good at the moment, but clarinets are up. Why worry?''[14]

CLASSICAL MUSIC AND OPERA

It was not only swing music that was attaining incredible popularity during the 1930s, but classical music as well. Dickson Skinner gave some startling figures in *Harper's Magazine* early in 1939:

In 1915 or thereabouts there had been 17 symphony orchestras in the United States. By 1939 there were over 270.

It was estimated that in 1938–39 the combined audiences on the air for the Metropolitan Opera on Saturday afternoon, the NBC symphony on Saturday evening, and the New York Philharmonic and Ford hour on Sunday, numbered 10,230,000 families *each week*. (Figure for yourself how many families had been able—and willing—to hear music of such calibre before 1930.)

Moreover, the Cooperative Analysis of Broadcasting had estimated the radio audience for the Detroit Symphony in 1937 at 118 percent higher than in 1935, and in 1938 it ranked fifth in national popularity behind only the news broadcast and three commercial programs. NBC was airing its Music Appreciation Hour in 1938 to more than 7 million students in some 70,000 schools, and its broadcasts of classical music and opera were averaging more than an hour per day.[15]

In 1938 swing and classical came together when Benny Goodman joined his clarinet with the Budapest String Quartet in a Victor album of Mozart's clarinet quintet. Its "best-seller eminence," *The New Republic* noted, was in part due to its "sort of freak quality" in featuring the "idol of swing" in recording such a work, but despite this feature, it opined that it was "a beautiful piece of recording all through."[16]

RECORDED MUSIC

The demonstrated popularity of classical music and opera over the airwaves quickly attracted commercial sponsors in the 1930s. And the radio broadcasts of both classical and swing music fueled a resurgence of interest in buying recorded music that breathed new life into a faltering record industry. After reaching a high of some 100 million phonograph records sold in 1921, the industry had declined as a result of the inroads of radio. Between 1919 and 1931, spending on phonographs and records plummeted from $339 million per year down to $17 million. By 1933 total sales of records were down to the level of 1907, but then the industry began to rebound. Between 1933 and 1938 the upward curve was almost identical with that of 1907–12, and in 1938 about 35 million records were sold. In fact, the best-selling Christmas gifts nationally in December 1938 were phonograph records. The reasons, *The Saturday Evening Post* concluded, could be traced to the popularity of the combination radio-phonograph, the portable phonograph, and swing music. More and more people were buying radio-phonograph combinations, rather than one or the other, while portable phonographs had become popular with youth and vacationers. The radio had created a wider appreciation for good music, but it had then driven music lovers away from it and to phonograph records because of "its overlong and blatant commercials."[17]

For those who could not afford to buy all of the tunes they desired, there was by late in the decade the accomodating jukebox that could be found in almost every restaurant, bar, or soda fountain. A nickel deposited in the slot brought forth the sound of the latest hit song. The combination of radio and records, however, cut sharply into sales of sheet music. Families in the 1930s were more likely to listen to music on the radio or from the record player than to play it themselves.

Outside the home, jukeboxes (or jookboxes, as they were sometimes spelled in the 1930s) offered the opportunity to play and hear the latest tunes in more and more locations as the decade wore on. The initial stimulus for jukeboxes came from the repeal of prohibition, which resulted in the opening of thousands of bars and taverns across the United States. People had grown accustomed during the 1920s to hearing music in their favorite speakeasies. It was a difficult habit to break, but it was clearly impossible to have live music in all of the new watering holes of the 1930s. The solution was obvious. Give the patrons pay-for-play phonograph players.

By the end of the decade an estimated 325,000 bars, restaurants, soda fountains, railway stations, excursion boats, and roadhouses sported jukeboxes, into which approximately 5 million nickels dropped each day, producing a $20 million per year industry that employed an estimated 100,000 workers. The Wurlitzer Company, leading manufacturer of jukeboxes (more than its next four competitors combined), reported a net profit for 1939–40 of over $1 million.[18]

The popularity of jukeboxes contributed immensely to the boom in record sales in the second half of the 1930s. With over 300,000 machines going through approximately 275 records per year, it is apparent that jukeboxes, alone, must have accounted for nearly 10 million in record sales annually. The tunes chosen for the jukeboxes, however, were not always the latest popular works. Many of them reflected local and ethnic tastes in the titles available: hot swing in Harlem, grand opera in Italian restaurants, country and western in the South, polkas in parts of the upper Midwest, Mexican music along the border, Oriental tunes in San Francisco's Chinatown, and even Yiddish platters in New York City.

Of course, the swing music of the second half of the 1930s was the most popular, and jukeboxes were credited with the rise to stardom of many bands and vocalists, including that of the Glenn Miller Orchestra. The success of Bonnie Baker's recording of "Oh Johnny, Oh" was said to be the primary reason for the rise of the Orrin Tucker orchestra (for which she was vocalist) from "the ranks of the second rate to a $10,000-a-week nightclub and vaudeville attraction."[19] Many novelty tunes attained popularity on the jukeboxes before they achieved any significant time on the radio waves. Royalties from the nickels inserted into the jukeboxes flowed into the pockets of more than 3,000 recording artists.

Some drinking establishments used "come on" girls to boost play on their machines, who sometimes danced with customers where that was permitted. In such cases the jukebox might be equipped with either a dime or quarter slot instead of the usual nickel one.[20]

MOVIES AS ESCAPE

Movies also contributed a great deal to the popularity of music and musicians during the 1930s. The union of sound and color early in the decade at first lent itself to the production of musicals, in which the two developments could be exploited to the maximum. Such movies, which frequently featured the rise of some unknown to stardom, furnished at least a few hours of escape from the realities outside the theater and kept alive the dreams of upward mobility during a time when most mobility was in the opposite direction. Musical productions were expensive, however, and as viewers began to decline the industry looked for cheaper forms to exploit, while featuring stars guaranteed to attract patrons. Even cheaper black and white productions, however, frequently featured scenes of musical groups and vocalists as part of the story line or as background.

Movies during the 1930s mirrored many of the trends in other aspects of the popular culture of the depression. The emphasis was on escape from the realities of the day-to-day struggle with economic conditions. For the most part movies continued to deal with light and entertaining subjects—musicals, romances, and comedies. As Frederick Lewis Allen observed, they revealed "hardly a glimpse of the real America," but rather "took one to a never-never land of adventure and romance uncomplicated by thought." Viewers of later decades, he wrote, who watched a random selection of a dozen or two movies from the decade, "would probably derive from them not the faintest idea of the ordeal through which the United States went in the nineteen-thirties."[21] For Louis Reid, the movie industry shared with radio the distinction of aiming its product at "the twelve-year-old mind." Americans, he wrote, attended the movies in the 1930s for the same reasons they listened to the radio, "either out of sheer habit or to pass the time or, as is most likely, out of a desire to escape monotonous, graceless reality."[22]

In her cross-country study of youth in the mid-1930s, Maxine Davis found that movies had become the "narcotic" of the young, because:

Life is empty; they lose themselves in a glamorous world where marvelous things happen.

Life is boring; the make-believe world is tremendously exciting.

Their tomorrows are like their yesterdays and todays; they run away from them in a gripping dream of adventure and romance.

Their lives are without color; in the movie palace they have the whole spectrum.

They travel to far places and backward into history, effortless as an opium smoker.

They identify themselves with Hollywood heroines. They love and anguish and struggle and succeed vicariously.

Movies, she wrote, were "nothing more nor less than an anodyne for the bleak today. Pay a dime or a quarter and buy a ready-made Elysium."[23]

There were, of course, some movies that touched on aspects of the unpleasant realities of the 1930s: Charlie Chaplin's *City Lights* (1931) and *Modern Times* (1936), and other major studio productions like *I Am a Fugitive from a Chain Gang* (1932), as well as a number of minor works. In general, however, as Dixon Wecter has pointed out, "the content of most motion pictures still was designed for escape, the majority reflecting the tastes of tired or jaded adults seeking a never-never land of luxury and melodrama, sex and sentiment."[24] There was, however, a subtle change induced by the depression. In 1932, for example, it was unlikely that a movie would portray its hero or heroine finding a quick and easy road to success, such as was the case in many 1920s movies. Instead, the road from rags to riches was now more likely to be depicted as a gradual triumph over adversity. In either case, however, the moviegoer was encouraged to have faith in ultimate success.[25]

The sex themes that had been tolerated in the silents of the 1920s were a good deal more realistic and provocative when pursued with the addition of accompanying dialogue in the talkies of the 1930s. As a result there was a reaction in the early 1930s against the overly explicit sexual themes that were increasingly common. The Legion of Decency, formed in April 1934 by Catholic bishops and Protestant allies, began to exert pressure on Hollywood to clean up its product under threat of possible boycott if it didn't. The major Hollywood studios quickly fell into line. There would be no more seduction scenes, no savage kissing, excess drunkenness, displays of people in their underwear, or use of such words as "louse" or "floozy." Clearly the industry had gone overboard, and there were soon complaints that the controls were too strict.[26]

Will Hays, president of the Motion Picture Producers and Distributers of America, described Hollywood's view of its function in depression America and his assessment of its value in his annual report of 1934. "No medium," he wrote, "has contributed more greatly than the films to the maintenance of the national morale during a period featured by revolution, riot and political turmoil in other countries." He continued: "It has been the mission of the screen, without ignoring the serious social problems of the day, to reflect aspiration, achievement, optimism and kindly humor in its entertainment."[27] The 1930s was the first decade in which two of the major technological developments of the movie industry—sound and color—were exploited. The novelty of these attractions cushioned the industry against the effects of the depression for the first few years. Patrons were at first willing to dig into their shrinking entertainment dollars to experience the new marvel. As the novelty wore off, however, and the depression lengthened, the movie industry joined the rest of the country in experiencing hard times. By mid-1933 nearly one-third of the nation's theaters had closed their doors.

MOVIE THEMES

In the early 1930s some movies began to draw on newspaper headlines for their inspiration, especially headlines dealing with crime. Gangster films attained wide popularity in these years, at the same time that the theme was invading the comic strips and radio dramas. Darryl Zanuck, in particular, exploited the theme successfully with such movies as *Doorway to Hell, Little Caesar*, and *The Public Enemy*. Gangster movies met the principal tests of the depression: they could be made cheaply, and their hard-hitting, fast-moving, masculine action attracted viewers.[28]

Some excellent movies were made during the 1930s, including such classics as *Mutiny on the Bounty, The Life of Emile Zola*, and *A Tale of Two Cities*, and a few that treated the problems of the 1930s, like *Gentlemen are Born* and *Wild Boys of the Road*. For the most part, however, films during the 1930s exploited the same tastes that were being filled by the fiction (and advertisements) in popular magazines like *The Saturday Evening Post*. Sophisticated comedies like *It Happened One Night, My Man Godfrey, Topper* and *The Awful Truth* abounded, featuring actresses like Carole Lombard, Jean Harlow, Mae West, Tallulah Bankhead, Constance Bennett, Marlene Dietrich, and Katharine Hepburn, and actors like James Cagney, Spencer Tracy, Gary Cooper, Fred MacMurray, Cary Grant, Melvyn Douglas, and David Niven. Comedians like the Ritz and Marx brothers and W. C. Fields carried that genre to the limits of slapstick in the 1930s. Such movies, Frederick Lewis Allen observed, portrayed "a country in which almost everybody was rich or about to be rich, and in which the possession of a huge house and a British-accented butler and a private swimming pool not merely raised no embarrassing questions about the distribution of wealth, but was accepted as the normal lot of mankind."[29]

The developments of color and sound were also ideal for transporting comics from the pages of newspapers to animated versions on film. The master of cartoon films was Walt Disney, who was probably more influential than any other filmmaker during the 1930s in cheering the American spirit during the depression. Tunes introduced by two of his movies inspired Americans at two of the lowest points in the depression and were widely whistled and sung: from "Who's Afraid of the Big Bad Wolf?" in *The Three Little Pigs* in 1933, to "Heigh-ho, Heigh-ho, It's Off to Work We Go" in *Snow White and the Seven Dwarfs* during the renewed downturn late in the decade. One historian of the cinema has written that *The Three Little Pigs* "helped to turn the tide of pessimism toward optimism and strengthened the hope that co-ordinated action would pull the country out of its slump."[30] Will Hays remarked that "historians of the future will not ignore the interesting and significant fact that the 'movies' literally laughed the big, bad wolf of depression out of the public mind through the protagonism of 'Three Little Pigs'—a screen favorite that overflowed to the radio, the public press and to millions of homes."[31]

Louis Reid found that the American of the 1930s "achieves his truest escape from reality, finds his heart most cheered, his imagination most stirred by the glowing figures of Mickey Mouse, Donald Duck, the Three Pigs, Dopey, and his dwarfish comrades." The Disney movies and characters, he wrote, had "been the greatest boon to the movies since sound."[32] The Disney characters spawned popular books and toys. The first Mickey Mouse watch appeared in 1933 and Macy's sold 11,000 of them in the first day of their release. A Three Little Pigs book designed for Christmas 1933 found 50,000 copies ordered before it was even published, and publishers could not keep up with the demand.[33] In the Department of Agriculture, however, officials attributed much of the unpopularity of the Agricultural Adjustment Administration (AAA) to the fact that Disney's *Three Little Pigs* had been released just before the AAA embarked on its infamous mass slaughter of piglets.[34]

The youngsters of many towns and cities in the 1930s were able to join Mickey Mouse clubs cosponsored by their local theaters and other businesses to stimulate attendance at Saturday matinees and teach good citizenship. By 1932 there were already over a million members in the United States, and there were branches in Great Britain as well. In 1933 the first official *Mickey Mouse Magazine* also appeared, at first sold through department stores that marketed Disney merchandise or in movie theaters that showed his films. President Franklin Delano Roosevelt and his wife Eleanor were devoted Mickey Mouse fans.

Two characteristics of the comic pages in the 1930s that were regarded unfavorably by some observers were true also of the movies. *Saturday Review*'s comments on comic strip violence could have been applied with even more validity to the movies. Violence in the movies was not restricted to the gangster and action pictures, where it would be expected, but was commonplace also in comedies and romances, which were often filled with pie-throwing, slaps, blows, and shoves. Such comedic violence was of course a staple of the exaggerated comedies of the Marx Brothers and others. And the animated cartoons of film were no less violent that their comic strip counterparts. Even Disney's cartoons were often filled with brutal, bullying behavior dished out by Mickey Mouse or another of the Disney characters.

Beginning with 1934, filmgoers could escape such violence and experience upbeat entertainment by attending the succession of Shirley Temple movies that won for her the hearts of Americans during the depression and after. Such movies as *Little Miss Marker, Baby, Take a Bow*, and *Now and Forever* (all 1934), *The Littlest Rebel* (1935), *Poor Little Rich Girl* (1936), and *Heidi* (1937) led President Roosevelt to remark: "During this Depression, when the spirit of the people is lower than at any other time, it is a splendid thing that for just 15 cents an American can go to a movie and look at the smiling face of a baby and forget his troubles."[35] Like cartoon characters, Shirley spawned a line of dolls, cutouts, books, and other products. Other child stars were popular in the 1930s, but none as much as Shirley, whose smiling inability to give in to adversity and her triumphs over seemingly insuperable obstacles were an inspiration for Americans.

Similarly, filmmakers in the 1930s did their part in trying to refurbish the image of businessmen (of which they were, of course, a part) that had been so tarnished in the public mind as a result of the prolonged depression and the accompanying revelations of misdeeds by businessmen and bankers. The image of businessmen and bankers portrayed in the movies was not far from that of Daddy Warbucks in *Little Orphan Annie*. As one film historian noted, businessmen were portrayed as "the man who works as hard as any of his laborers, . . . who has struggled hard for success and must continue struggling to keep it. He is beset with financial worries, labor problems, personal disappointments. Like the banker, the corporation executive is depicted as a leader fighting single-handed to help the people."[36]

NEWSREELS

A major development in the film industry of the 1930s, which broadened its competition with newspapers and radio, was the introduction of newsreels, beginning with the *March of Time* in 1934. Newsreels proved enormously popular. Although they could not be as current as the newspapers or radio, they offered the visual appeal that radio lacked and the newspapers and newsmagazines could offer only through still photographs. Their popularity can be seen in the fact that by the 1930s some theaters were devoting themselves exclusively to newsreel presentations.[37] Not until the flowering of television news beginning with the 1950s could Americans obtain such graphic images of world events and figures as were obtainable in their movie theaters.

COPING WITH HARD TIMES

The film industry embraced and exploited trends, fads, and crazes during the 1930s just as avidly as did other entrepreneurs and the public at large. In the early 1930s, in fact, there was even a brief attempt to copy radio in introducing "commercials." As one study described it, "radio broadcasting, with its 'sponsored' programs, had habituated the public to vocal advertising; when the talking picture appeared, its employment in a similar manner was an obvious corollary.'' The opposition of newspapers and magazines, however, led to the abandonment of "sponsored" movies soon after they were begun.[38]

Early in the 1930s the owners of first-run theaters found that the depressed economic conditions were cutting into their audiences. As incomes fell, people chose cheaper second-, even third- or fourth-run theaters in order to stretch their budgets. First-run theaters faced a choice of either reducing their prices or playing to empty houses. When they reduced their prices it naturally forced reductions all down the line, making it difficult for all but the second-run theaters to continue in business at the lower prices they were forced to charge, and many had to close their doors.

Theater owners also began to look for alternatives or supplements to reduced ticket prices that would attract patrons. Double features, which had formerly been shown only by smaller neighborhood theaters, were now adopted by even first-run houses. In addition, theaters offered games like bingo, with premiums and cash prizes, as well as amateur nights and giveaways like cheap radios. On certain normally slow nights, individual pieces of china or tableware were given to women, so that by steady patronage a complete set might be accumulated. One of the most popular inducements was Bank Night and its many imitators.

Bank Night, like so many fads and crazes of the 1930s, originated in Colorado. It was invented by Charles Urban Yeager, assistant division manager of the Rocky Mountain division of Fox Theaters, and first introduced in theaters in Delta and Montrose, Colorado, in the winter of 1932–33. It quickly became so popular that Yeager quit his job, copyrighted Bank Night, and franchised it to theaters all across the country. By 1936 nearly one-third of American theaters had adopted it. Bank Night worked simply. Theater patrons wrote their names in a large book in the lobby. Numbers next to their names coincided with numbers on tickets kept in the box office. On Bank Night—usually Monday or Tuesday, since these were typically slow nights—the winning ticket was drawn from a drum on stage by a child and the winner was allowed three minutes to claim the prize (usually $150 to begin with) on stage. If the winner did not appear, the prize was increased and the drawing was repeated a week later.[39]

By the end of 1937 it was estimated that at least 100 million persons had participated in Bank Night drawings, and that each week more than 5,000 theaters were distributing almost $1 million in prizes. Forbes Parkhill wrote in *The Saturday Evening Post* that ''it's got to the point where nobody can schedule a basketball game, a church sociable or a contract [bridge] party on Tuesday night,'' because everybody was at the local theaters hoping to cash in on Bank Night. So large were the crowds that most people had to stand in the street because not all could pack into the small theaters. Bank Nights, he wrote, had "profoundly affected the social life of America," and were especially "a headache to the traffic squads." The brewery trade was not happy, either, one of its journals having complained that the public was spending its money on Bank Nights instead of on beer![40]

Bank Night made it possible for theaters to run unpopular movies to packed houses on off nights without violating antilottery laws, since the patrons did not buy lottery tickets. Yeager's copyright was, however, easily avoided by imitations using other names, and its use spread beyond movie theaters to retailers and even to New York's popular night spot, the Stork Club. In Des Moines, Iowa, Bank Night was so popular that the police and fire departments had occasionally to be called out to control the crowds.[41] Clearly Bank Night and its imitators were symbolic of the general get-rich-quick preoccupation of Americans during the 1930s as seen in so many of the fads and crazes of the decade.

THE THEATER

Professional theater could have used such innovations during the 1930s. Faced with shrinking entertainment dollars because of the depression and the competition of radio and movies, theaters closed and shows failed in the early 1930s. Vaudeville, especially, suffered its final agonies. Amateur theater took up some of the slack and enjoyed rapid growth in the 1930s, producing plays for an estimated audience of 15 million annually by 1940. Meanwhile, the New Deal had moved to succor actors and other theater workers through federal theater projects that brought their productions to an audience estimated at 20–25 million people, many of whom had probably never seen a play before. Many of the productions glorified the New Deal and others went beyond into even more left-wing pastures, in both cases arousing opposition from those who did not expect that federal appropriations would be used for such blatant propagandizing. As a result, Congress cut off appropriations for the project in 1939 and it closed.

Commercial theater during the 1930s offered a mixture of the traditional sophisticated comedies, "message" works criticizing capitalism, war, and, later, totalitarianism, and satires on the Hoover and Roosevelt administrations, as well as works on folk themes. One effect of the depression and the competition of radio and movies was a rapid decline in the number of traveling companies that had once brought Broadway shows to small towns, with the result that commercial theater began to reach a much smaller audience and one that was geographically limited to a few major cities. Its audience could not compare with the millions who watched movies and the many more millions who obtained their entertainment from the radio.[42] Commercial theater had, in short, become but a minor factor in the popular culture of America by the end of the 1930s.

AN AMERICAN ART

Curiously, while commercial theater declined, other arts were experiencing a popularity rarely seen even in prosperous times. "America," wrote one observer in the 1930s, "has become American art conscious."[43] During few decades in American history has art been so much a part of popular culture as it was during the decade of the Great Depression. In large part this resulted from the fact that a great many artists during the decade devoted themselves to portraying or interpreting the American scene instead of aping European trends that, however prized they might be by critics, had little appeal for typical Americans.

Martha Candler Chenery wrote in 1939:

In the relatively short time that has elapsed since 1925 America has come into the possession of a voluminous native subject art. We have an exhaustive summation of our own epoch in terms not only of New York City's teeming life, but of the life of Pittsburgh, Chicago, Cleveland, Detroit, Los Angeles, and the rural areas of the Midwest, the Dust Bowl and the flood and tornado areas, the agricultural far South, Alaska, and the Virgin Islands.

The unprecedented spending on art works in the prosperous years of the late 1920s had contributed greatly to the trend, providing "unheard-of opportunites for American painters." In 1928, alone, American art investments reached $1 billion.[44]

The market for a more realistic art based on American sources attracted many painters in the late 1920s. The stock market crash of 1929 and the depression that followed deprived such artists of the patronage they had experienced before the crash. At precisely the time that painters of the American scene were becoming most appreciated, the majority of the public lost the ability to buy their works. The depression also brought changes in the mood and character of the works painted. The dominant American style through much of the 1930s was the so-called American Scene, as exemplified in the works of artists like Grant Wood, Thomas Hart Benton, John Steuart Curry, Charles Burchfield, and Reginald Marsh. Their paintings represented the Midwest (Missouri, Iowa, Kansas, and Ohio) and New York City.

Benton explained the credo of American Scene painters in a speech of 1932, when he said:

No American art can come to those who do not live an American life, who do not have an American psychology, and who cannot find in America justification for their lives. . . . American art can be found only in the life of the American people; and there will be no background for its development until art itself comes out of its cultural enclosures and produces goods which have meaning for the American people.[45]

Grant Wood explained that each area of the United States possessed its own personality, and "thinking painters and writers who have passed their formative years in these regions will, by careful analysis, work out and interpret in their productions, these varying personalities.[46]

Benton was known mainly for murals of American life in which he accentuated the picturesque or grotesque features of his figures in the turbulent scenes where they were set. Wood is remembered for his Iowa portrait studies, such as *American Gothic*, in which he was painstakingly explicit in his details. In part, one observer suggested, his works' popularity derived from the 1930s fascination with cartoons, since Wood's *American Gothic* was "something of a cartoon," while Benton's characters were "active and heroic in a restless comic strip way."[47] Burchfield's work in the 1930s was mainly in landscapes, while some of Curry's most famous work in the decade was a spectacular group of canvasses that resulted from his travels with the Ringling Brothers Circus. Marsh dealt with a variety of subjects, including the burlesque theater, crowded subways, and bathing beaches—wherever common people gathered.

Although labeled the American Scene school, the painters did not comprise any sort of organized group. Nevertheless, their success led many other painters of lesser talents to try to emulate them, even as the same painters had rather pathetically tried to ape every other popular trend. As Cheney wrote: "One of the most spectacular evidences of their appeal (and one of the most unfortunate and confusing circumstances, from the point of view of critical appreciation) is the numbers of painters and students who became American Scenists almost overnight." Or, as one art critic put it, "all the little four-flushing Picassos turned into little Bentons and little Grant Woodses."[48]

Popular culture and art came together, also, in the regional art movement that flourished in the 1930s. Regionalism, which centered around regional art showcases, colonies, and schools, found expression in nearly every part of the country, fostering distinctive regional styles. Typical of such regionalism was that of New Mexico, centered around Santa Fe and Taos, where artists created a distinctive style that included "the intensity of the light, the color on desert mountains, the effects of space and distance, the life of the aboriginal peoples there." Many of the regionalists gained national reputations and popularity for their work. In their best works the regionalists joined painters like Wood and Benton in creating a uniquely American modern art.[49]

As in literature, some radical painters of the 1930s sought to create a proletarian art by taking advantage of themes of class exploitation and repression with a zeal that, like that of their writer equivalents, was not shared by the public at large and that, therefore, was limited in its impact on public culture. It was, wrote one historian, "our first widespread outspoken movement of pictorial social criticism," and included many left-wing viewpoints but at its core was the Marxist belief that art is meaningless except insofar as it promotes the class struggle. Such "propaganda" art dealt melodramatically with strikes, starving workers, breadlines, police brutality, lynchings, and other such themes.[50]

Another factor in the popularization of art during the 1930s was the federal patronage given artists during the New Deal years. Alice Marquis noted that such patronage had resulted in "a prodigious flood of art in America," including more than 2,500 murals of one form or another, 18,000 sculptures, and 110,000 easel paintings, and half a million photographs. In addition the federal government encouraged and furnished support for over 100 community art centers. The result was not only more artists (many of them of doubtful talents) and art works (many of them of dubious quality), but also a larger audience for art.[51]

Summarizing the art achievements of the decade in 1939 Cheney concluded that

America can no longer be called a nation without the capacity to make an art of her own. We have such an art, and there are two orders of accomplishment by which it may be judged.

We have a large pictorial and sculptural record of American life, rich in regional and human diversities of character and in the thought, feeling, and idealism of the people. This broadly representative popular record in painting and sculpture is significant because it affirms a new relationship between artist and society, of a kind and on a scale that this country has not known before and that has been little known in any country in recent centuries.

We have also, among the producers of this art, or side by side with them, the always necessarily smaller number of true creators of high rank, who are demonstrating their power of independent aesthetic expression and are giving us, in the terms of their own original experience, works that are worthy to stand with the abiding art products of past periods.[52]

And that American art had been contributed by painters whose names reflected the great diversity of America's ethnic groups: Asian, European, Latin American, and Native American.

"The painters of the American scene opened our eyes to all those things from which the older genteel generation had averted their gaze," wrote Lloyd Goodrich. "To them we owe a visual discovery of America equivalent to the literary discoveries of Dreiser, Anderson, Lewis, Faulker and Wolfe."[53]

DESIGN

In design, Art Deco continued to dominate through the first half of the 1930s, as it had during the 1920s. It found its inspiration in exotic countries like Egypt, and in technology, and its influence spread to affect the design of virtually everything, utilitarian and nonutilitarian alike. In its rejection of historical precedents it was particularly adaptable to new elements in American culture like radio and automobiles. As one authority has put it, "so ubiquitous was Art Deco that it might be regarded not merely as a form of taste but as a way of life, roughly spanning the years from 1920 to 1935."[54] In mid-decade, Art Deco was superseded by what people of the 1930s referred to as streamlining, or as Industrial Art Moderne. Its influence gradually spread from the galleries during the early 1930s until it had reached virtually every American home by influencing the design of everything from buildings to furniture to bathroom and kitchen fixtures to radios and toasters. The new designers, says one source, "maneuvered their aesthetic into every corner of society." Traditional crafts gave way to those manufactured by machines using new materials like aluminum, bent tubular steel, and the new plastics. The result was "a new, growing consumer ethic in the middle of the Depression." The interiors of homes, offices, and stores became showcases of the new Industrial Art Moderne, as were the skies, the railroad tracks and the highways, for the new breed of designers were also streamlining airplanes, locomotives, buildings, buses, automobiles, even ocean liners.[55]

"Manufacturers," *Editor and Publisher* remarked early in 1935, had since 1929 "given great attention to design." The contributions of artists and designers had resulted in "added beauty, efficient performance, and economical operation undreamed of in the 'golden years.' "

The depression has given America graceful airplanes that regularly span the country between dawn and dusk; railway trains that weigh pounds to their predecessors' tons and run for pennies against dollars; automotive power which can banish the ancient bogy of a gasoline shortage within present lifetimes; beautifully designed automobiles fabricated almost in one operation by presses which make 1929 machines look like stone-age toys; almost instantaneous transmission of news photographs over limitless areas; fabricated steel structures which may solve the low-cost housing problem; air-conditioning in office, home and railway train; scientifically designed home-heating equipment that combines comfort with economy; household machinery which adorns its surroundings, while adding to the leisure time of wives and mothers.

All of this, and more, had been accomplished "while the United States has been supporting 15 to 20 per cent of its population on relief rolls."[56]

CHAPTER SIX

Sports

THE DEPRESSION AND SPORTS

Athletics was, sportswriter John Tunis wrote in the early 1930s, "today the religion of the United States," with its own set of idols, "the true gods of the nation." Sports heroes like Babe Ruth and Bobby Jones and Bill Tilden were "the saints of the great American national religion; the religion of sports."[1] How better to distract oneself from the realities of the depression than to enter with thousands of others into the temporary trance of a few hours of sports fanaticism?

Depression pocketbooks inevitably cut attendance at some sports events, especially in the early years of the depression, but *Literary Digest* observed late in 1933 that the business of having fun seemed to be experiencing a recovery even if not much else was. Attendance at college football games was up that fall. A Princeton-Amherst game had attracted 20,000 fans, and the same number had watched Kansas tie Notre Dame; 60,000 watched as California downed St. Mary's, and 40,000 had seen USC devour Washington State.[2] The University of Hawaii had a fair football team in the 1930s, but they had little success winning games when they ventured to the mainland. They tried to overcome the disadvantage of not having their cheering section with them when they played at UCLA in 1935 by making phonograph records of their fans cheering in Honolulu, and then playing them during the game in Los Angeles. Unfortunately, it didn't help. The Washington *Post* wrote that they "should have sent the entire student body to Los Angeles to cheer personally, and recruited their football team in Pittsburgh."[3]

COLLEGE FOOTBALL

So popular was college football, especially, during the 1930s, that by 1938 there were already complaints that there were too many postseason bowl games. Originally there had been only the Rose Bowl, but by 1938 it had been joined by the Orange Bowl (1935), the Sun Bowl (1936), the Sugar Bowl (1937), and the Cotton Bowl (1937), as well as the shorter-lived Eastern Bowl and Coal Bowl.[4]

One reason for the increased popularity was doubtless rule changes made during the 1930s that encouraged more passing. In 1934 the circumference of the ball was reduced, making it easier to grip for passing, and the existing five-yard penalty for more than one incomplete pass in the same series of downs was eliminated. Later in the decade penalties were added for passing to an ineligible player and ineligible players were prohibited from advancing beyond the line of scrimmage on a pass play. As a result, the 1930s saw a wider-open offense, especially in the Southwest, and the development of some of the greatest passers of all time, including Sammy Baugh (Texas Christian University) and Sid Luckman (Columbia) who would go on to pass the National Football League (NFL) silly.

As in the past, there were numerous awards for outstanding coaches, players, and teams, but the 1930s saw the beginnings of two notable such awards: the Knute Rockne Trophy, emblematic of the "national championship" at the end of the season, and the Heissman Trophy, for the outstanding player of the year. USC won the first Rockne trophy in 1931, climaxing a 10–1 season that included a victory over Notre Dame and a Rose Bowl victory over Tulane. The 16–14 come-from-behind victory over Notre Dame (then known as the Ramblers) snapped their 26-game unbeaten streak. Other teams, not known today as national football powers, fielded notable teams in the 1930s. Columbia went 7–1 in 1933 and then defeated Stanford in the Rose Bowl, 7–0. Minnesota lost only one game between 1934 and 1936. In the latter year the Associated Press began its poll ranking the nation's college football teams, and Minnesota was voted the number 1 team in the nation.[5]

Alabama in 1934 featured one of the greatest ends in the history of football—Don Hutson—who went on to professional football fame. At the other end was a player who would go on to distinguish himself as football coach at Alabama—Paul "Bear" Bryant. The first Heissman Trophy was awarded in 1935 to Jay Berwanger: star runner, passer, kicker, and defensive player for the University of Chicago. In that year Southern Methodist University won the Rockne Trophy and went on to be the first southwestern team to play in a major bowl game when they were invited to the Rose Bowl. En route they had to defeat a powerful Texas Christian University (TCU) team, led by one of the greatest passers of the 1930s, All-American Sammy Baugh, 20–14.

A Big Ten team, the University of Minnesota, won the Rockne Trophy in 1936, even though Northwestern beat it out for the conference championship. Eastern football was distinguished by Fordham—which fielded its famous "Seven Blocks of Granite" in 1937, a defensive line that allowed only 16 points in its eight games—and by successive Heissman trophy winners from Yale University in 1936 and 1937. In the latter year Clint Frank of Yale won it over Byron "Whizzer" White of the University of Colorado, who led the nation in rushing, total offense, and in scoring with 16 touchdowns and 23 extra points. White played almost 60 minutes of every game—defense and offense—punted and place-kicked, and even rank back kick-offs and punts. He led Colorado to an undefeated season, a conference championship, and an appearance in the Cotton Bowl—the first appearance in a bowl game ever for a team out of the Rocky Mountain area. White was probably the greatest collegiate football player of the 1930s, and without a doubt the greatest *scholar*-athlete. In addition to All-American honors in football, White was also all-conference in both basketball and baseball, a Phi Beta Kappa and a Rhodes Scholar.

Davey O'Brien won both the Heissman and Maxwell awards at TCU in 1938 with his flawless quarterbacking and excellent passing, and led his team to the national championship and a victory over Carnegie Tech in the Sugar Bowl. Tennessee was close behind TCU in the national rankings with an unbeaten season and an Orange Bowl victory over Oklahoma. Duke had the distinction in 1938 of not giving up a single point in its nine games before losing to USC in the Rose Bowl 7–3 on a last-minute touchdown pass. Texas A & M kept the national championship in the Lone Star state in 1939, with an undefeated season and a Sugar Bowl victory over Tulane. Among the other powerhouses of 1939 was UCLA, which went through it first undefeated season ever. The Bruins featured two outstanding black halfbacks: Kenny Washington, who went on to a distinguished career in the NFL, and Jackie Robinson, who later became the first black to play major-league baseball.

College football had allowed radio broadcasts of its games for several years before professional baseball permitted it. By 1932, however, colleges were having second thoughts, convinced the broadcasts were cutting into their gate receipts by encouraging potential spectators to stay home and listen to the games on radio. The loss of gate receipts, in turn, put the continued existence of minor sports in peril. The Southern Conference, made up of 23 colleges and universities, banned radio broadcasts at the end of the 1931 season, and the Eastern Intercollegiate Association—which included Yale, Harvard, Princeton, Pennsylvania, Brown, Pittsburgh, the Army and Navy academies, Columbia, Syracuse, and Dartmouth—followed suit in 1932. The Big Ten conference was opposed to radio broadcasts and other conferences also considering banning them. Radio's representatives naturally opposed the action, and argued that radio stimulated interest and thereby attendance at games rather than reducing it. *Literary Digest* wondered, however, if many fans had not come to the conclusion that

it is more fun to sit beside a cozy fire with an invigorating beverage in one hand and a mellow pipe in the other, and take in their stride as much football as they conveniently can out of the ether, than to freeze on a hard concrete seat and juggle a flask while drunks climb on their necks, scream in their ears, and make it impossible to enjoy the game?[6]

Four years later college games were back on the air. Public demand for the broadcasts had created interest among commercial sponsors who were willing to pay the colleges and universities for the right to broadcast their games. College football would now, H. I. Phillips wrote, "be a fellow worker with Eddie Cantor" and other radio entertainers, while "the bowls and stadia in the year 1936" had become "handmaidens of the broadcasting studio." Phillips added:

When the university elements slam one another around, this autumn, they are doing it not only for the glory of Alma Mater but for the advancement of American industry, the promotion of high-powered salesmanship, and in support of general business recovery. Every call for the ambulance is a contribution to radio suspense, and every broken bone a highlight in air-wave entertainment.

Yale was the first to accept a contract, receiving $20,000 for the rights to broadcast six games, and Yale's decision was quickly followed by "a rush of American colleges to cash in on radio rights in which the rules against elbowing, jumping, hurdling, and roughing the runner were thrown to the four winds." It was, Phillips wrote, "one of the great stampedes of history," which ended with 24 colleges and universities inking commercial contracts for broadcasts of their games.[7]

With the exception of football, however, spectator sports in the 1930s declined from their so-called golden age in the 1920s and the sports heroes of the 1930s did not seem as heroic as those of the previous decade. Some of the heroes of the 1920s, like Babe Ruth and Red Grange, were still playing in the early 1930s, but the best years of their careers were clearly behind them. Each sport in the 1930s had its stars, but few approached Ruth and Grange in winning the adulation of fan and nonfan alike that they had enjoyed in the previous decade.

BASEBALL

Professional baseball, for example, did not do as well in the early 1930s as college football in attracting fans. The New York *Herald Tribune* suggested in mid-1939 that perhaps the solution to the problem of poor attendance was to begin playing major league baseball games at night. Night baseball had been first tried officially in Iowa in 1930, but Westbrook Pegler found that it had only resulted in the fans being eaten by mosquitoes.[8] Nevertheless, Cincinnati introduced night games in 1935 and the ploy was successful in bringing out the fans. Despite their opposition to the idea, other teams were forced to follow suit for economic reasons and night baseball turned red ink into black for a number of teams in both leagues. Team owners also copied from movie theater owners by offering doubleheaders, but this made fans feel cheated when they got only one game for the price of a ticket.

Declining attendance and reduced receipts meant that expenses had to be cut somewhere, and players' salaries were an obvious place. In 1933, even Babe Ruth was forced to take a $23,000 cut in pay, from $75,000 to $52,000, and all of the other members of the Yankees team likewise had to take pay cuts.[9] Only attendance at World Series games seemed unaffected by the depression. Minor league teams and players were affected even more than the major leaguers, and of course ex-players also suffered. The first major league all-star game was held in 1933, in association with the Chicago World's Fair, in order to provide money for indigent ex-ball players. It became an annual event.

To try to increase interest in baseball, the teams began to allow radio broadcasting of their games, beginning with the St. Louis Cardinals in 1935. The newspaper industry was not pleased with this development. Fans would no longer have to read newspapers to find out what had happened in the game. *Editor and Publisher* magazine whined that after these many years during which newspapers had publicized the sport and sustained it, the baseball teams were turning their backs on the press and snuggling up to the radio stations.[10]

The American League began the 1930s as it ended the 1920s, with Connie Mack's Philadelphia Athletics taking the championships from 1929–31. The A's also took the World Series in the first two years, but lost to the St. Louis Cardinals in seven games in 1931. The Yankees bested the Cubs in 1932, and the Giants then captured the title for the National League in 1933 by beating the Washington Senators. The Cardinals triumphed over the Detroit Tigers in 1934, but the Tigers came back in 1935 to win the title from the Chicago Cubs.

In 1936 the New York Yankees began an incredible string of four straight American League and World Series championships, beating their intracity rivals the Giants the first two years, and then sweeping the Cubs and Reds in four straight games in 1938 and 1939. Combined with their 1932 victory, it meant that the Yankees took five of the ten World Series in the 1930s. It was a good decade for the American League, which also won five all-star games in the 1930s to two for the National League.

The Yankees were easily the best team of the decade, and the team of 1938 was probably one of the best of all times. Ruth was the major league home-run leader in 1930, and tied with teammate Lou Gehrig in 1931. Gehrig went on to win the home-run championship in 1934 and 1936, with 49 in each year, and Joe DiMaggio of the Yankees won it in 1937. The 1938 Yankees included Gehrig in his last full year, DiMaggio, Bill Dickey, Joe Gordon, the two "Reds"—Rolfe and Ruffing—, Frank Crosetti, and George Selkirk, with the immortal Lefty Gomez the mainstay of the pitching staff.

Another outstanding team of the decade, and perhaps the most colorful of them all, was the St. Louis Cardinals of 1934. They were, says one baseball historian, "a rough and ready outfit, with a chip on their shoulders and wings on their feet, hungry for victory and its rewards, and chock full of confidence and disrespect for the opposition."[11] This was the team managed by Frankie Frisch that included Pepper Martin, Ducky Medwick, Leo "the Lip" Durocher, Rip Collins, and the inimitable pitching combination of the Dean brothers, Dizzy and Paul. Dizzy Dean became a colorful legend in his own time. The two brothers won a total of 96 games over two season, with Dizzy reaching 30 victories in 1934—the first time that plateau had been reached since 1917. Major league baseball did not lack for colorful figures during the 1930s.

The 1930s also saw the beginning of Little League baseball, when Carl E. Stotz organized the first three teams in Williamsport, Pennsylvania, in 1939. The program, with the opportunity it provided for boys to compete on teams in organized leagues, quickly spread not only through the United States but overseas as well.

THE RISE OF THE NATIONAL FOOTBALL LEAGUE

The National Football League began the 1930s as it had ended the 1920s, with the Green Bay Packers as champions, 1929–31, of a league that included teams like the Providence (RI) Steamroller, Frankford (PA) Yellowjackets, Portsmouth (OH) Spartans, and Brooklyn Tigers. In 1932 the Chicago Bears captured their first title in 11 years, with a 9–0 indoor victory (because of subzero temperatures) over Portsmouth, played in Chicago Stadium with the goal lines only 80 yards apart and the cement floor of the stadium covered by a layer of turf left over from a benefit circus that had just played the arena. The Bears' attack featured the young Bronko Nagurski and the veteran Red Grange, who combined for the winning touchdown.

Passing the football was difficult before 1931 because its "cantaloupe" size and shape reduced accuracy. In 1931 the pro ball was slimmed by a half-inch, and in 1934 it was trimmed by another full inch. Meanwhile, in 1933 the NFL altered its rules to permit passing from anywhere behind the line of scrimmage. The combination of these changes opened the game up to more passing and made it more exciting. Passers and pass receivers now became headline players. The first of the great receivers was doubtless Don Hutson of the Green Bay Packers, a former Alabama collegiate player.

The League was also divided in the 1930s into two divisions—East and West—with provision for the two division champions to play for the NFL championship. This format continued until the merger of the NFL with the American Football League and the creation of the National and American Football Conferences, with their own geographic divisions. New York, Brooklyn, Boston, Philadelphia, and Pittsburgh were in the East, while the West consisted of the Chicago Bears and Cardinals, Portsmouth, Green Bay, and Cincinnati. The New York Giants and Chicago Bears won the divisional races and met in the first NFL playoff game on December 17, 1933, at Wrigley Field, Chicago, before 26,000 fans. The Bears won a thriller, 23–21, when a tackle by Red Grange stymied the Giants in their last scoring opportunity. Those were the days, of course, when players went both ways—playing both offense and defense. Each player for the Bears received $210.34 as the winners' share, while the Giants received $140.22 each.

In 1934 the Bears participated in the first ever game between the NFL champions and the College All Stars. During the depression years, charity games were not uncommon. The Giants played one in 1930 against a team of former Notre Dame stars coached by Knute Rockne that provided over $115,000 for New York City's unemployment fund. The 1934 College All Star game was the brainchild of Arch Ward, sports editor of the Chicago *Tribune*, who conceived it as a charity match in connection with the Century of Progress Exposition in Chicago. The game drew nearly 80,000 fans to Soldier Field who watched the Bears struggle to a scoreless tie with the collegians.

In 1934 the Providence franchise moved to Detroit, where it became the Lions, and later in the year the Cincinnati club moved to St. Louis. The Bears beat off a challenge from the Detroit Lions to win the division and went into the NFL playoff against the Giants once again. That playoff was, Harold Claassen writes, "one of pro football's strangest contests."[12] Bitter cold and a frigid wind greeted the players when they trotted onto the icy field of the Polo Grounds on December 9, 1934. Footing would obviously be a problem, since the frozen turf was as hard as concrete. The Giants' coach, Steve Owen, immediately sent people in search of sneakers for his team to wear. By the time nine pairs of sneakers arrived, stolen from the lockers at Manhattan College, the Bears were ahead 10–3. With all the Giant starters clad in sneakers except their center and one guard, the New York team staged a rally in the final quarter, running around the slipping and sliding Bears to score 27 points for a 30–13 victory. It was Red Grange's last season.

Inclement weather during the 1936 season kept attendance at NFL games down, and the same was true on the day of the NFL championship game. On a snowy afternoon at the University of Detroit stadium, the Detroit Lions ripped the Giants 26–7. At its annual meeting two months later, the NFL instituted the player draft, which is still a major feature of professional football. The purpose was to give weaker teams the first opportunity to hire the best college players by setting the order of the draft in inverse order to the teams' standings the previous season.

In 1936 the Green Bay Packers took the West and the Boston Redskins the East. Boston fans did not get to enjoy their championship, however, as Redskins owner George Preston Marshall was thoroughly disgusted with the city. He moved the championship game to the Polo Grounds in New York, and then, after the Redskins lost to the Packers 21–6, Marshall moved the Redskins franchise from Boston to Washington, DC.

In their first year in Washington, the Redskins unveiled one of the genuine heroes of the game and arguably the greatest professional football player of the 1930s. This was a lean all-American halfback from Texas Christian University named Sammy Baugh, who would, Claassen writes, "pass the league dizzy in a phenomenal 16 seasons of stardom." With Baugh throwing the ball, the Redskins won their second straight Eastern championship, trouncing the Giants 49–14 on the way. After a successful year for the NFL, in which nearly 1.2 million fans attended games, the Redskins met the Chicago Bears for the championship at Wrigley Field in Chicago. Trailing 21–14 going into the fourth quarter, "Slingin' Sammy" went to work, throwing touchdown passes of 78 and 35 yards to give the Redskins a 28–21 victory. Baugh's record for the day: 17 completions out of 34 attempts for 347 yards and 3 touchdowns.

Despite Baugh's heroics for the Redskins, the 1938 championship game matched the Green Bay Packers from the West with the New York Giants representing the East. Attendance at NFL games continued to rise, increasing 15 percent over the healthy attendance of 1937. And a record championship game crowd of 48,120 turned out to watch the Giants take the title with a 23–17 victory. The Packers, however, revenged themselves the following year when the championship game matched the same two teams, this time at the Milwaukee State Fair Grounds before over 32,000 fans. The game was a rout, with the Packers winning 27–0.

By the end of the 1930s, the NFL had progressed far beyond its status at the beginning of the decade. The common impression that the quality of pro play was inferior to that of the collegians was dispelled by the Giants' victory over Rockne's team of ex-Notre Dame stars, and the respectable NFL record in the College All Star games from 1934 onward. Rule changes had made the professional game more exciting (the colleges did not allow passing from anywhere behind the line until 1945). NFL teams were now attracting some of the best collegiate players, whereas in the 1920s the professional game had been regarded as less than savory by many college players. And the NFL franchises were now, with the exception of the one in Green Bay, Wisconsin, located in major metropolitan market areas where they were attracting sizable crowds. Moreover, by 1939 the NFL had star players like Sammy Baugh, who were major attractions, and others recently recruited who would make their greatest impact in the 1940s, including Sid Luckman who came to the Bears in 1939 from an illustrious college career at Columbia University. As early as 1934, Will Rogers warned college football coaches that they had "better open up your game for this pro game was just made for an audience."[13]

BASKETBALL

Professional basketball did not attain nearly the level of popularity in the 1930s reached by its football counterpart, and would have to await the postwar years and the formation of the National Basketball Association before it would attract significant fan interest. College stars were as likely to play with the strong American Athletic Union teams of the 1930s, such as the Phillips Oilers, perennial national champions. But college basketball underwent a metamorphosis in the 1930s that changed it from a comparatively boring interlude between football and baseball seasons into an exciting sport in its own right.

When the 1930s began, basketball was slow-paced and dull. Scores on the order of 17–15 were not uncommon in college games. There was no ten-second time limit for bringing the ball across half-court, and a center jump followed every field goal scored. Teams might stall for a good part of a half, sometimes not bothering to bring the ball from under their own basket. During such stalls some players on a team might actually sit down on the court. Two such games in 1932 led to the adoption of the ten-second clock. In a game against UCLA, Southern California held the ball for the last 15 minutes of the first half. One of its star players read the newspaper, and outraged fans showered the court with pennies and peanut shells. In a Missouri-Kansas game the same year, four players on each team actually sat down.[14]

The ten-second clock speeded up the game, brought more fast breaks, and more sophisticated offenses and defenses. The standard shot, however, was still the two-hand set shot and free-throws were generally shot underhand. And there was still the delay in play caused by the center jump after each field goal. That was eliminated, finally, during the 1937–38 season, and the action heated up, the pace quickened, and scores mounted. The modern game of basketball had arrived by 1938 and the fans showed their appreciation.

A major impetus to the rise in popularity of college basketball also came from the promotion skills of a young newspaperman named Ned Irish.

Irish interested the president of Madison Square Garden in a proposal under which he would promote college basketball games at the Garden. Under the agreement reached, Irish obtained a virtual monopoly on college basketball played at the Garden as long as he met the agreed upon minimum of $4,000 per night. On December 29, 1934, Irish promoted his first game, between New York University and Notre Dame, and attracted over 16,000 fans. During the remainder of the 1930s the major basketball powers vied with one another for the right to play at the Garden, which was now in the spotlight of college basketball. In 1938 he promoted the first National Invitation Tournament. The following year, the National Collegiate Athletic Association began its own national championship tournament, which was won by the University of Oregon.

Easily the outstanding basketball star of the 1930s was Stanford University's Angelo Enrico "Hank' Luisetti. Luisetti has been hailed as the first "modern" basketball player and as the first "star" of the sport. As one writer has noted, it "was not so much that he shot, rebounded, dribbled, passed and played defense better than anyone else, but that he did almost all these things in unorthodox ways. He dribbled and passed behind his back, and he appeared to shoot without glancing at the basket." Above all, Luisetti was known for his running one-hand shot. He made the All-American team three years in a row, was named College Player of the Year twice, led Stanford to three straight Pacific Coast Conference championships, and broke the four-season collegiate scoring record. After graduating from Stanford, Luisetti passed up a lucrative pro offer to join the Phillips Oilers.[15]

GOLF

In golf, the 1930s began with the Grand Slam victory of Bobby Jones in 1930 and his retirement as a player after that triumph. From the distance of over a half-century it is not easy to understand how an amateur golf player could become perhaps the preeminent hero of the golden age of sports, the 1920s. How many golf players—amateur or professional— receive ticker-tape parades through the skyscrapered canyons of New York City, as Jones did in 1930 when he returned from his triumphs in both the British Amateur and Open golf tournaments? Was Jones' popularity in part because he was often the underdog—the amateur battling the professionals? Or was it because in the materialistic 1920s, Jones was an example of a man who shunned materialism and played for the sheer joy of the game?

Jones' return from his British triumphs in 1930 was followed by his victories in the U.S. Open and Amateur, which meant that he had completed the nearly impossible task of winning what was called "The Grand Slam"—sweeping the four major tournaments in the United States and Great Britain that were open to amateurs. That accomplishment, Frederick Lewis Allen wrote, "inspired more words of cabled news than any other individual's exploits during 1930," including the World Series, the successful U.S. defense of yachting's America's Cup, or any other news story.[16]

Jones, however, celebrated his 1930 triumph by announcing shortly thereafter his retirement from tournament golf. Fans were shocked. As one historian of the game wrote of the reaction: "Golf without Jones would be like France without Paris—leaderless, lightless, and lonely."[17] It would, also, for a time, be profitless, for the U.S. Golfing Association was losing its star attraction at the same time that the depression, too, had begun to reduce the size of the galleries.

Individual country clubs also suffered from the depression, when the reduced incomes of golfers made it difficult for them to keep up the expensive dues and fees. Many country clubs were forced out of business; others became public courses by selling out to their municipalities or states; still others were forced to take in members they would have earlier shunned, either as regular members or in new membership categories created to help them survive. Herbert Warren Wind noted that golfers "who had formerly belonged to two or three clubs now had to save up before blowing themselves to a round of miniature golf."[18] For club professionals whose clubs had gone under, earnings on the tour now became a necessity.

No other golfer in the 1930s attracted the attention and acclaim of Bobby Jones, but other noted golfers did appear in the decade. Gene Sarazen, who, as a professional, had labored in Jones' shadow during the 1920s, won both the British and U.S. Opens in 1932 and also fashioned the first sand-wedge late that year. Lawson Little first came to American attention in 1934 as a result of his performance on the U.S. Walker Cup team and his victory in the British Amateur, and he followed up these feats with a victory in the U.S. Amateur that year as well. In 1935, Little successfully defended both his British and U.S. Amateur titles, becoming the only golfer to have ever won both championships in consecutive years.

The second half of the 1930s benefited from improvements in golf equipment and courses, both of which contributed to a lowering of scores. And in 1937, Wind wrote, "professional golf graduated into Big Business." When Fred Corcoran became tournament director of the Professional Golfers Association in 1936, he went to work promoting more tournaments and larger purses. He also promoted the golfers, themselves, into well-known personalities. And in 1937 and 1938 Slammin' Sammy Snead began to set the golf world afire. By the late 1930s golfers like Snead and Byron Nelson, who would be headliners in the sport in the 1940s and 1950s, were making their mark.

The participation of Americans in international sports competitions like Wimbledon in tennis has always fascinated the public and it was no less the case in the 1930s. Mention has already been made of the ticker-tape parade for Bobby Jones when he returned from winning the British Amateur and Open golf tournaments in 1930. In addition to such events for individuals there were already in the 1930s the three golf cup competitions that matched American and British teams: the Walker, Ryder, and Curtis cup events. The Walker Cup was for amateur players, the Curtis Cup for women players, and the Ryder Cup was for professionals. The Curtis Cup began in 1932, and was held four times during the 1930s, with U.S. women winning three times and tying once. American amateurs likewise dominated the Walker Cup competition during the decade, losing it only in 1938, but the Ryder Cup was won by the host country at each competition, except in 1937 when the Americans won overseas.

TENNIS

The situation in tennis was much like that in golf. As Bobby Jones had retired from amateur golf in 1930, thus depriving it of its greatest hero, so did Bill Tilden, the greatest name in tennis, give up his amateur standing the following year in order to turn professional. Tilden's departure left the spotlight to new emerging tennis players like Ellsworth Vines and Don Budge among men players, and Alice Marble in women's tennis. Vines appeared from nowhere in the early 1930s, lit up the tennis sky briefly, and then was gone. In 1931 and 1932 he won at Forest Hills and was the number 1 ranked tennis player in the world. He was hailed as the successor of Big Bill Tilden and promoters were offering him handsome contracts to turn professional. Vines, however, decided to wait a year, and he had a disappointing 1933, losing in the final at Wimbledon and playing poorly in the Davis Cup competition. Vines then turned professional and toured with Tilden. He was the undisputed pro champion until 1939 when Don Budge took charge, whereupon Vines took up golf and made it his life's passion.

Don Budge came on more slowly, lasted longer, and accomplished more. He had not yet become a star when he was invited to join the U.S. Davis Cup team in 1935. The United Stated had not won the Davis Cup in nearly a decade, and the new captain wanted to replace the team with younger players. Nevertheless, Budge did not hit his tennis stride until 1937. In that year he helped the United States win the Davis Cup for the first time since 1926, then won the U.S. Nationals. He turned down professional offers and in 1938 he reached the pinnacle of tennis by winning the Australian and French championships, taking Wimbledon, and defending his U.S. Open title, thus becoming the first Grand Slam winner in history—an honor that not even the great Bill Tilden had achieved. And in the midst of it all he had helped the United States to defend its Davis Cup with two wins against the Australians. Now Budge turned professional. There were no more worlds to conquer.

Among women players, Helen Wills' name had become a household term by the end of the 1920s, although she also went by her nickname, "Little Miss Poker Face." Wills won seven U.S. women's titles between 1923 and 1931, losing only in 1926 because of an appendicitis attack. She won Wimbledon from 1927 to 1930, and also in 1932, 1933, 1935, and 1938 (at the age of 32, after three years of virtual retirement). She turned down a lucrative professional offer and spent the rest of her life as a writer of mystery novels and tennis books, a painter whose work was exhibited in galleries throughout the world, and a fashion designer.

Her place was taken by Alice Marble, a farmer's daughter from California, who won the first of four U.S. championships in 1936 and captured the Wimbledon title in 1939. In the process she was one of the first women to wear boyish shorts at both Forest Hills and Wimbledon. She was voted outstanding woman athlete of the year in 1939 and 1940. A serious illness, however, ended her career in the latter year.

THE OLYMPICS

There is, of course, no international competition like the Olympics games, and the United States hosted both the summer and winter Olympics in 1932—the summer games in Los Angeles, and the winter games at Lake Placid, New York. Despite the depression, the state of California and the city of Los Angeles combined to make a spectacular success of the 1932 summer games, and Americans crowded to the stadia and arenas in numbers that established an Olympic record to match the many new ones that were being set by the participants. An average of over 60,000 spectators attended each day, far exceeding the attendance at any previous Olympics. Gate receipts exceeded a half-million dollars, establishing yet another record.

American men won 11 of the 23 track and field events, including victories in the 100- and 200-meter dashes by Eddie Tolan, a black runner from Detroit who raced with horn-rimmed glasses taped to his ears. Tolan was the only winner of two gold medals.

The Olympics performance of the 1930s that is best known today, however, is undoubtedly that of Jesse Owens in the Berlin Olympics of 1936, not only because of Owens' accomplishment but also because of the drama surrounding the success of an American black athlete in shattering the myth of Nordic superiority that Adolf Hitler and his underlings were trying to propagandize. Owens repeated Tolan's victories in the 100- and 200-meter dashes, and added a victory in the running broad jump. He also ran a leg for the gold-medal-winning 400-meter relay team. American blacks also finished first and second in the high jump, and won the 800 meters and 400 meters, finished second in the 100- and 200-meter dashes (behind Owens), all of which only furnished further discomfiture for Herr Hitler. The American swimming team also triumphed in Berlin, after losing to the Japanese in Los Angeles despite two gold medals in the 100 and 400 meters by Helene Madison. In 1936 the male swimmers and divers did better than the women's team, perhaps in part because Eleanor Holm Jarrett, winner of the backstroke in 1932, was disqualified from the team en route to Europe for breaking training aboard ship.

American boxers fared better in 1932 when they won gold medals in the welterweight and middleweight categories, than in 1936 when they won none at Berlin. There was a similar decline in gold medals in free-style wrestling, and Americans won no gold medals in weightlifting in either Olympics. Taking all events into consideration, the United States dominated the 1932 Olympics with 104 medals (41 gold) to only 36 (12 gold) for Italy, their nearest competitor. It was the fourth straight Olympic win for the United States. In 1936, however, the German hosts at the Berlin Olympics posted 89 medals (33 golds) to eclipse the second-place Americans' 56 (24 golds).

The Winter Olympics at Lake Placid, New York, in 1932 was an incredible Olympics for the American team. Americans won as many gold medals (6) in 1932 as total medals four years earlier at St. Moritz, and more than their total medal count (4, 1 gold) at Garmisch-Partenkirchen four years later. Their 12 total medals gave them a sizable victory over second-place Norway, whose 10 medals included only 3 gold. Two brothers from Lake Placid, Hubert and Curtis Stevens, aged 41 and 33, won the two-man bobsled, attributing part of their success to the fact that they heated their runners with blowtorches before the race (now illegal). An American team also won the four-man bobsled race. One of its members, Eddie Egan, became the only Olympian to win gold medals in both summer and winter Olympics. He had won the light-heavyweight gold medal in boxing in 1920 at Antwerp. Neither U.S. men nor women fared well in figure skating at Lake Placid, but Americans fell in love with the Norwegian winner, Sonja Henie, who went on to a successful movie career in the United States after winning the gold medal again in 1936. The United States picked up its remaining gold medals at Lake Placid in speed skating, when John Shea swept the 500- and 1,500-meter events, and Irving Jaffee took the 5,000- and 10,000-meter golds.

Despite all of these heroics, however, the greatest Olympic performer of the 1930s, and arguably the most accomplished athlete of the decade, was a woman—Mildred "Babe" Didrikson. Other athletes, male or female, might master a sport or two, but there seemed to be almost nothing in athletics at which Babe Didrikson could not excel. In the 1932 Olympic trials in Chicago she won 11 events. She was allowed to compete in only three in the Olympic Games at Los Angeles and she won the 80-meter hurdles and set a new world record in the javelin throw. She would probably have won the high jump, or at least gained a tie, except that a judge objected to her unorthodox style of jumping. How many more gold medals might she have won if she had been allowed to represent the United States in all 11 events for which she qualified at the trials?! She could also play basketball, tennis, polo, football, soccer, lacrosse, pool and billiards; and she could swim, dive, golf, and throw a baseball and football. In the late 1930s she began to concentrate on golf and she quickly became one of the leading women golfers in the United States, a position she retained for many years. The great sports writer Paul Gallico described her as "unquestionably the greatest all-around athlete this country has ever produced." There had never been a man, he added, "who could do half the things she can in sports, or do them as competently."[19]

BOXING

Professional boxing suffered from a loss of fan interest after the retirement of Gene Tunney in 1928, but it was rejuvenated by the arrival on the scene of the greatest pugilist of the 1930s, Joe Louis, the Brown Bomber, who captured the world heavyweight championship in 1937 from James J. Braddock. Arguably the greatest fight, however, especially for the rags-to-riches story it embodied for Americans seeking hope in the depression, was the victory of Braddock over Max Baer for the championship in June 1935. Braddock, an unemployed longshoreman, had been on the relief rolls only a year before he won the championship. After Louis captured the championship from Braddock in 1937 there were no serious challengers for the crown, and fan attention once again began to decline.

SOFTBALL

After decades of minor interest, from its creation in 1888, softball—a kind of miniature version of baseball—assumed the dimensions of what *Time* magazine described as a "mania" beginning with 1930. Although no one could explain its sudden popularity, the sport seems to have offered at least two attractive qualities for the times. For one, it could be played at night when depression-era families had time on their hands and sought low-cost diversion. While the lighting of even major league baseball fields was still in its infancy, the smaller size of softball fields made them easier to light, even at the sandlot level. And the smaller size of the field and other variations on baseball made it easier for women, too, to participate in the sport.

By 1935 there were an estimated 2 million softball players organized in some 60,000 amateur teams belonging to one of two national softball associations: the American Association, headed by former major league first baseman, George Sisler; and the National Association, headed by a former baseball player and sportswriter named Philip Rosier. Softballers played on over 1,000 lighted fields, most of them located in the Midwest. Softball entrepreneurship was a lucrative pursuit. Fields seating 4,000 fans could be built for approximately $3,500, and with crowds of over 1,000 paying a dime each for admission they could pay for themselves in a month.[20]

By 1939 the number of softball players had mushroomed to more than 5 million players and a half-million teams, with numerous semiprofessional teams among both men and women, and with a softball world's series. Women's teams were especially popular among male spectators because of the abbreviated shorts they wore.[21]

THE SKIING CRAZE

The skiing craze of the 1930s is not as easy to understand as those for miniature golf and softball. As Frederick Lewis Allen pointed out, it was an inexpensive pastime for those who lived in skiing areas, but an expensive one for those who did not. Allen suggests that it might have been the outgrowth of a new vogue of winter holidaying. Or perhaps those who had in the 1920s motored to the warmer climes of Florida during the winter could no longer afford to do so and headed for the ski slopes, instead. Whatever the reason, the new interest in skiing seems to have been an outgrowth of the 1932 winter Olympics held in Lake Placid, New York. Railroads began operating special ski trains to the slopes and their success led others all over the country to inaugurate similar train and bus services. Department stores found sales of ski equipment prospering, and some imported Norwegian specialists to give advice to tyros.[22]

CHAPTER SEVEN

Style and Life

FASHION AND INFORMALITY

Herbert Hoover's tall, stiff, detachable shirt collar had already, by inauguration day in 1933, become more suited for wear in England than in the United States. The transition from Hoover's uncomfortable collar to the soft shirt collar of Franklin Delano Roosevelt meant that the trend toward comfort and less formality in men's wear had finally reached the White House. Hoover's collar had become as thoroughly discarded as the former president himself.

The 1930s brought to fruition a trend that had begun at least a decade previous, away from what Newman Levy called "the Age of Discomfort" to the "Age of Comfort." "All the stiffness of apparel," he wrote, "has vanished, and with it much stiffness of manner." Levy wrote:

Frequently my father wore a silk hat and a cutaway coat downtown. Today that costume is reserved for afternoon weddings and Tammany Hall funerals. It is strange to recall that he used to address many of his fairly close friends, men whom he had known for years, as Mister. Among my friends the first-name habit is universal. The man who does not call you Jack, Tom, or Dick after a half hour's acquaintance is generally regarded as pompous and rather high-hat. All of this can be directly attributed of course to the current habit of wearing soft collars. With it has come a new juvenility of spirit.[1]

One evidence of the new informality in dress was the beginning of topless bathing on New York beaches in 1936 by men. Some women, however, objected to the sight of hairy-chested men, and at least one club posted a notice by its pool requesting "all male members having hair on their chests to refrain from swimming in the club pool without bathing shirts."[2]

Walter Pitkin found in the early years of the 1930s that men were spending less on clothes and shoes, while women were spending more. Men, he said, preferred to spend their money on travel and other pleasures if forced to make a choice.[3] Thus, men's wardrobes began to eschew not only the stiff collars of the 1920s, but also hats, garters, undershirts, and vests, while new purchases of suits and other essential items of attire were delayed.[4]

One fad among women in the early 1930s was feathered Empress Eugenie hats, which they wore everywhere. Paul Sann recalled: "There never was a flash fire like that one in the millinery industry before—or since. While it was raging, the world wasn't safe for ostriches, turkeys, ducks, geese or even the lowly pigeon." Ostrich feathers were preferred, but when they became scarce and expensive, "American manufacturers took dead aim on the barnyard fowl in their own backyard." Some 4,000 women worked in 300 factories in New York at the height of the boom. Then, within a few months, the fad died. Women not only stopped wearing feathered hats, they stopped buying any hats at all, thereby throwing the millinery industry into a panic.[5] The fashionable woman also began to paint her fingernails in bright colors, and by the early 1930s the fad had spread even to sales clerks and typists.

As in the 1920s, housewives copied the styles of Hollywood stars like Ginger Rogers and Deanna Durbin. In the 1930s this meant that the typical woman visited her local beauty salon regularly for an "electric permanent" to fashion her hair after that of her Hollywood favorite. In the first half of the 1930s bobbed hair was popular again, although not cut as short as in the flapper style of the 1920s; and in the second half of the 1930s the pageboy or curled bob reaching to the shoulder became fashionable. Women also copied the clothing and shoes worn by favorite stars in their latest movies. The practice became so prevalent in the 1930s that manufacturers and retailers were alerted in advance of the specific items of apparel that popular stars would be wearing in their next movies so that production could begin before the movies were released in anticipation of demand. One shoe manufacturer reported that whenever a certain star wore a new style of shoes it was necessary "to change our shoe pattern to conform, which means an expenditure of many thousands of dollars. Every time a new picture is released a new style is created and there is an instantaneous demand for it from women in all parts of the country."[6]

Thus, when Maxine Davis traveled cross-country she found that the average girl in the 1930s was looking to Hollywood for her fashions, rather than, as in the 1920s, to high society. Instead of aping the Vanderbilts and Whitneys, girls now modeled their hair, clothes, and manners after the Norma Shearers and Constance Bennetts. So pervasive had the practice become throughout the country that "Park Avenue and Four Corners look just about alike. The girls on both thoroughfares get their ideas and their patterns from the same animated models!" The result was that American girls were "quite attractive, though they're all exactly alike."[7]

In their study of college students in the 1930s, Bromley and Britten found that the "dark shadows cast by the depression" had affected collegiate fashions.

Overnight the college man banished coonskin overcoats, bell-bottomed trousers, cute mottos on his automobile, all the "rah-rah" gestures. Men and women students dress with a new sobriety. In the eastern colleges which set the fashions for the Middle West, the girls are dressing with the studied simplicity of the smart set. They wear sport clothes, sweaters and skirts, ankle socks, low-heeled comfortable shoes, no hats. The men have adopted the English fashion of wearing coats and trousers that do not match.[8]

In general, women's waistlines rose to their waists again after sliding downward during the 1920s, and hemlines fell low enough to conceal the legs before rising again in the mid-1930s. Otherwise, women's clothes were designed to conform to the body's natural contours.[9]

Those contours grew rounder in the 1930s, as the slim, boyish look of the 1920s passed from vogue. The Washington *Post* wondered if the new trend might not be a boon to the nation's economic recovery: "A little plumping of the ladies at this time might rescue the farmer. A new deal in contour might whirl the wheels of the great textile industry." A five-pound increase of weight for each of the 60 million women in America translated into a total of 300 million pounds. Farmers would prosper in producing the additional butter, grains, cream, and other foods necessary for all of those pounds. At the same time, the trend toward longer skirts would help to revive the textile industry. Who needed the New Deal?![10]

THE INDISPENSABLE AUTOMOBILE

Curiously enough, in their return to Middletown midway through the decade the Lynds found that the depression had least affected the business of gas filling stations, whose sales had fallen only by 4 percent and whose number had almost doubled in the first four depression years. This was eloquent testimony of the love affair that Americans continued to have with their automobiles even in depressed economic times. "People," the Lynds were continually told, "give up everything in the world but their car." Car ownership, they found, "was one of the most depression-proof elements of the city's life in the years following 1929—far less vulnerable, apparently, than marriages, divorces, new babies, clothing, jewelry, and most other measurable things both large and small.'' People were riding in progressively older cars as the depression went on, but they continued to ride, and it was estimated by a local paper that some 10,000 Middletonians were leaving the city every Sunday to visit other towns and resorts.[11]

The "Sunday driver" precedent had already been established by the late 1920s when magazine stories hailed the benefits to mind and health that accrued from a one-day-in-the-week spin to the countryside or from town to town. The automobile had, in short, become a principal source of recreation for Americans by the beginning of the 1930s. As Foster Dulles observed:

For countless millions the automobile was for the first time bringing the golf course, tennis court, or bathing beach within practical reach. It made holiday picnics in the country and weekend excursions to hunt or fish vastly easier. It greatly stimulated the whole outdoor movement, making camping possible for many people for whom woods, mountains and streams had formerly been inaccessible. It provided a means of holiday travel for a people always wanting to be on the move.[12]

As the 1930s began, a writer in *Vanity Fair* found: "On every thoroughfare and country lane, on highway and byway, up and down the length and breadth of our native land, America is spending its Sabbath day on wheels." Lined up "bumper to bumper" with "radiators pressed to spare tires," they looked "like an interminable file of circus elephants with their tails in their trunks."[13]

In part this mobility was made possible by the relative cheapness of gasoline, which sold for about one-third of the cost in Europe at about a nickel-and-dime per gallon. Moreover, automobiles became much more comfortable and dependable during the 1930s. Not only were they an improvement over earlier automobiles, Bernard De Voto wrote, but his 1934 vehicle's dependability was positively "utopian" in comparison "with other household developments of the machine age, the refrigerator, the vacuum cleaner, the oil-heater (above all, the oil-heater!)."[14] Most automobiles were closed models during the 1930s, making winter travel almost as convenient as that during the summer, and not only the automobiles themselves were more dependable, but also the tires and other necessities for automobile travel.[15] The addition of dashboard radios in the 1930s meant that travelers did not even have to miss their favorite radio programs while driving. But, despite the new features introduced during the 1930s—ventilators; sloping radiators; free-wheeling; streamlined "airflow" design; hydraulic brakes; and gearless shifting—most

Americans were determined to get as many miles out of the old "bus" as possible during the depression.

Americans in general clearly were taking to the road. While travel to foreign countries dropped by nearly 45 percent between 1930 and 1933, 300,000 Americans still traveled abroad in the latter year, and in 1937 that number had grown by nearly 50 percent—back to the level of 1926.[16] But the greatest growth in travel by Americans that is measurable statistically was to national parks and monuments. Visits to these (including national historical parks) rose steadily during the depression, and leaped by nearly five times between 1929, the last nondepression year, and 1939.[17] Clearly Americans had begun to rely principally on their automobiles for their vacation travel, and during the 1930s every part of the country vied for the vacation dollars of American travelers through glowing magazine and newspaper advertisements promoting their mountains, seashores, or open spaces. The slogan was "See America First."[18]

WORLD'S FAIRS

One attraction for domestic travelers was the variety of world's fairs held in the United States during the 1930s, which showcased American art, architecture, technology, fashion, and design. That Americans would invest in such elaborate projects in the midst of a depression, reflecting the pride and optimism that they implied, is yet another example, perhaps, of their unwillingness to accept the realities of their condition during the 1930s. Yet one motive for most of the fairs was the hope that they would contribute to tourism and economic recovery, at least in the part of the country where they were held.

The first of the world's fairs of the decade was the Chicago "Century of Progress," held in 1933–34 to celebrate the centennial of the city. The fair, built on the shores of Lake Michigan, emphasized the new ultramodern futuristic architecture that was capturing the imagination of the country's architects and designers. For many fairgoers this was their first exposure to the amazing new trends. The fair also spotlighted electricity, with "the world's largest display of electric lighting up until that time," a display that was activated by a beam of light from the star Arcturus. Exhibition halls featured the advances and applications of science and technology, and the midway featured such not-to-be-forgotten experiences as the famous fan dance of Sally Rand and the bumps and grinds of an aging Little Egypt. The combination of attractions drew about 10 million visitors in its first season.

In 1935 San Diego hosted the California Pacific Exposition in an effort to stimulate economic recovery in that area of the country; and the next year featured both the Great Lakes Exposition and the Texas Centennial

Exposition. They were followed by the Golden Gate Exposition that opened on an island—Treasure Island—specially constructed for the fair in the middle of San Francisco Bay. The San Francisco fair was held to commemorate the completion of the Golden Gate and Oakland Bay bridges and tended to play down modernism and technology somewhat.

The premier event of the 1930s, however, was clearly the New York World's Fair, held in 1939–40 on a 1,216-acre site in Flushing Meadow, and subtitled "The World's Greatest Showcase." It opened on April 30, 1939, to commemorate the 150th anniversary of the inauguration of George Washington as first president of the United States. The exhibits exposed many Americans to their first glimpse of a television set, and to the prospects of space travel. The exhibition halls were designed by America's leading industrial designers, and included the Trylon—a 700-foot obelisk with a connecting Perisphere, a hollow ball 200 feet in diameter that contained a diorama of a planned community of the future. The principal theme of the fair, ironic in view of what was happening in the world even as it was held, was "Building the World of Tomorrow," with a focus on the interdependence of man and the need for peace. Twenty-two foreign nations occupied pavilions surrounding the Court of Peace. Transcontinental railroads took advantage of the existence of the two world's fairs simultaneously being held on opposite coasts to offer excursion rate fares to those who wanted to see them both.

Obviously the New York World's Fair had as one of its objectives the separation of large numbers of people from their money. While it may not have been a "rich man's fair," as some charged, the admission fee and other prices within the fair were far from cheap. Moreover the fair, itself, and many of the corporations exhibiting within the fair, did a lucrative business in souvenirs, with the Fair Corporation alone licensing 900 manufacturers to produce 25,000 different souvenirs using the Trylon and Perisphere. These products ranged from armbands to zipper pulls, and buttons to umbrellas.

The amusement and entertainment areas included such spectacles as "Bring 'em Back Alive" Frank Buck's Jungleland, a Macy's Toyland, a Gangbusters Building, a dance center that featured a Harlem jitterbug show, and a 250-foot parachute jump. Former Olympic swimming stars Eleanor Holm and Johnny Weissmuller were featured in Billy Rose's Aquacade. Nothing would be seen like it again until the construction of Disneyland and its competitors later in the century.[19]

THE LANDSCAPE OF AMERICA

Writing late in the 1930s, Douglas Haskell described the changes that had taken place in the nation's highways in the past decade. They were no longer "mere connecting links from town to town," but were now "lined with structures." "At night," he wrote, in thickly settled areas such as northern New Jersey, they make driving one continuous battle against blare. Gas stations, Socony, Gulf, Sunoco, Texas [Texaco], or name your favorite brand. Gas stations with "lubritoriums," and announcements of "inspected" rest rooms. Gas stations with lunch rooms and tourist cabins. Harry's diner, surrounded by huge Diesel-powered trucks and trailers whose drivers are inside exchanging information on the whereabouts of the different inspectors. Paradise Dance Hall, whose parking lot explains itself. But the majority of the groups are straight "cabin camps" ministering to the ubiquitous transient called the "tourist."[20]

Accommodations for automobile travelers during the 1920s had usually consisted of little more than campgrounds, often established by a municipality, where tents could be pitched for a cheap and convenient overnight shelter. Minor conveniences like picnic tables and running water were provided. The number of these gradually declined during the decade as entrepreneurs developed better tourist accommodations, including cabins or cottages, and offered more services to travelers.

By the early 1930s these roadside auto camps were beginning to offer many of the services of a hotel, such as maid and porter service, and, as one advertised, "every convenience of a first class hotel." Another advertised that it was "a complete community, with drug store, barber shop, post office, grocery and meat market; paved street and side walk. 48 splendid furnished bungalows, plastered, complete plumbing, baths, gas ranges, screened porches, car shelters and comfortable furnishings, highly restricted. . . . Full hotel service. One of the finest cottage camps in U.S.A."[21] Clearly such "cottage camps" offered all the conveniences of home, including a kitchen, in addition to the desirable services of a hotel. Unlike the hotel, however, one did not have to enter through a lobby and therefore worry about one's appearance. Each cabin had its own entrance. And travelers did not have to worry about dressing for dinner at a restaurant, or the expense of dining out. If they stayed at a camp with kitchens in their cabins they could stop at a local market for groceries and cook in their cabin.[22] By the late 1930s this synthesization of hotel with tourist camp would reach completion with the emergence in the western states of the first motels.

Walter Pitkin wrote that the American traveler saw "little save huge, gaudy billboards advertising all the commonplace things he uses at home." The American highway, he concluded, was "the ugliest spot on earth."[23] One result was that the towns the American traveler visited in the 1930s were likely to be pretty much the same as his home town, and, as Elmer Davis wrote, "those that are not like it subtly begin to undergo a change under his influence, so that wherever he goes he may feel at home."[24]

The skylines of cities and the roadsides traversed by travelers became increasingly Art Deco in the 1930s, especially after the onset of the New Deal. Civic buildings, museums, schools, bus terminals, railroad stations, department stores, and chain stores all began to incorporate aspects of Art Deco in their design and/or decoration. Automats, too, were often designed in Art Deco, and were another example of America's use of coin-operated machines in the 1930s. Elaborate neon signs also began to hawk wares during the 1930s.[25]

THE PARKING METER

Increasingly as the 1930s progressed, one feature that the traveler was likely to find in whatever town or city he visited was a less-desirable form of nickel-gobbling machine than the kinds that were so popular as fads during the decade. Thanks to Carlton Cole Magee, a former Scripps-Howard newspaper editor who had been instrumental in unraveling the Teapot Dome oil scandal of the 1920s, the "automatic nickel-in-the-slot parking regulator" was sprung on an unsuspecting America in the mid-1930s. An Oklahoma City study into parking problems revealed that 80 percent of the cars parked in the busy downtown district belonged to employees who worked there, leaving insufficient parking for shoppers and others with business downtown. Magee thereupon invented the parking meter to discourage such long-term parking.[26]

Although bitterly opposed by the American Automobile Association, these "shoulder-high hitching-posts surmounted by nickel-devouring meters" spread quickly from Oklahoma City, where they were first installed, to ten other cities by 1936, including Dallas, Miami, and Kansas City, where a total of 8,702 Original Magee Park-O-Meters were taking in an average of 40 cents per day each on an investment of $58 per machine. Magee had a force of 300 field salesmen broadcasting the benefits of his machines as both parking regulators and sources of income for depression-impoverished city coffers.[27] The parking machines took only nickels, but the amount of parking time purchased for that amount varied according to the street. In the busier districts a nickel might buy only 10 or 15 minutes of parking time, but in most areas it bought an hour. One problem encountered in Miami was the tendency of owners of pint-sized Austin automobiles to park two of them in the one space alloted for a full-sized car![28] The story was told of one intoxicated man who mistook a parking meter for a jukebox and complained to a policeman when he didn't get any music for his nickel.[29]

As automobiles proliferated on the streets and highways of America and drove greater distances at higher speeds, the nation watched approximately 40,000 die annually in automobile accidents while over a million others were injured. Four million reprints were distributed of an article,

"—And Sudden Death," written by J. C. Furnas for *Reader's Digest*, in hopes that it would frighten drivers into safer habits, but there were nearly 2,000 more accidents in the following year, 1936, than in the year the article was written. After reaching a record high in 1937, the accident rate fell slightly for the rest of the decade, due perhaps to stiffer law enforcement and campaigns against drunk driving.[30]

MOBILE LIVING

Simultaneously a product of American nomadism and a contribution to hazardous traffic conditions in the 1930s was the rise of the travel trailer. Frederick Lewis Allen credits the invention of the first such mobile home to a bacteriologist named Arthur G. Sherman, who in 1929, just before the depression, "had built for his family a little house on wheels which could be towed behind his car on vacations." The favorable reaction caused him to begin building and exhibiting more until before long he and other manufacturers were busy building them for an expanding market, and home handymen were building them for themselves from plans readily available in popular magazines. By 1936 an estimated 160,000 were on the road, and on New Year's Day an estimated 25 were crossing the Florida state line every hour.[31]

For depression-era travelers they seemed to offer an alternative to the cost of lodging in hotels and dining in restaurants. A measure of the popularity of travel trailers as dream and reality can be seen by the fact that at least five books on trailer life were published in the year 1937 alone.[32] Some 700 manufacturers were involved in the trailer business at one point or another during the 1930s, not to mention countless unemployed carpenters and small machine shops who thought they had found a way out of the depression.[33] By the summer of 1938, however, the novelty had begun to wear off and sales of trailers slumped.[34]

For many, however, the mobile home was not just for travel. It was, instead, a substitute for the fixed home, an escape from being tied down by home ownership to one locality and one job, and freedom from real estate taxation. The result was that the 1930s saw the beginnings of "trailer towns," the ancestors of our modern mobile home communities. One of the leading advocates of the "mobile house" was Buckminster Fuller, who provided the new industry with a number of "guiding concepts" that would soon begin to influence their design and construction: prefabrication, reductions in weight, and streamlining, among others.[35]

OTHER FORMS OF TRANSPORTATION

Buses, too, began to be streamlined by the late 1930s, and throughout the decade were a low-cost alternative to other types of travel. The number of passengers nearly tripled between 1933 and 1941. In an effort to attract travelers back to the rails, railroads began to adopt air conditioning in their Pullman and coach cars to make travel more comfortable. The railroads also adopted the use of Diesel engines, lighter weight metals, and streamlining to make their most important runs faster and more attractive. The advances in railroad streamlining spread rapidly to automobile, truck, and bus design, as well.

The greatest transformation in transportation, however, occurred in the air. Before the 1930s, the great majority of Americans who had flown had done so only on short "thrill" rides offered by barnstorming pilots for the novelty. The depression initially caused a downturn in aircraft production, but by the second half of the 1930s the business had rallied, partly as a consequence of important technological advances during the decade. Meanwhile, New Deal work relief programs had built or improved thousands of air strips across the country. The major development was the Douglas DC-3 aircraft, which first flew in 1937 and was the first plane capable of making a profit from flying passengers alone. By the end of the decade air travel had become an option chosen by some 3 million persons annually, who flew over 120 million miles.

SHIFTING TASTES AND ATTITUDES

Frederick Lewis Allen, author of studies of both the 1920s and 1930s, wrote perceptively of the latter decade:

Looking back, one notices various contrasts between the social climate of the nineteen-twenties and that of the nineteen-thirties; and one notices, too, that most of these changes did not become clearly marked until about the year 1933, when the New Deal came in and the Eighteenth Amendment was repealed. It is almost as if the people of the United States had walked backward into the Depression, holding for dear life to the customs and ideals and assumptions of the time that was gone, even while these were one by one slipping out of reach; and then, in 1933, had given up their vain effort, turned about, and walked face-forward into the new world of the nineteen-thirties.

And did so, he might have added, with a beer or cocktail in their hands.[36]

The shifting standards and values of the 1930s were alluded to in Chapter One. Writing in the mid-1930s, a Jesuit wrote in *The Catholic World* that "in the loftier regions of human activity our superenlightened age has either abandoned all objective norms or taken unto itself false and foolish ones. In morals and in literature standards seem to have bidden a troubled world *adieu*, and few there are who mourn the loss." A great deal of attention, he wrote, had been given to America's departure from the gold standard in 1933, but little had been said of the millions who had gone "off the moral standard." The Ten Commandments had become objects of ridicule, "the religious prohibitions of a dead Moses." The new morality was the practice of the "art of living," without such shackles as principles, sanctions, or standards. As Mary Roberts Rinehart, the prominent author, put it: "There is no such word as sin in the old sense. . . . the decisions as to what is right and wrong lies with the individual and nowhere else."[37] In her talks with young people, Maxine Davis found them without discipline and following their impulses. "Without religious or social checks," she wrote, "indulgence is normal and restraint is unnatural."[38]

Not surprisingly, scholars found that American morale had suffered as a result of the depression. Edward C. Lindeman, professor of social philosophy at the New School of Social Work, wrote that as a result of the depression, "we are not motivated by confidence, we are split into numberless groups, cliques and parties struggling against each other and there does not exist a sufficiently large group deeply attached to a cause to make fundamental reform possible." Americans, he wrote, were awed by the complexity of modern civilization, a complexity that few were aware of until the depression revealed just how powerless they were over the situation. Youth, especially, had gone through a profound change in their attitudes toward life. Lindeman wrote: "If we divide youth generations into half-decades, this is what seemed to me to have happened:

1920–25: "Let's go!" Implication: Exuberance, recklessness, lack of direction.
1925–30: "Oh, yeah?" Implication: Distrust, lowered energy.
1930–35: "So what." Implication: Loss of purpose, disbelief, cynicism.

Youths, he found, were still skeptical about the future.[39]

In her study of what she called "The Lost Generation," Maxine Davis noted that the depression years had left America "with a generation robbed of time and opportunity just as the Great War left the world its heritage of a lost generation." She wrote:

Our young people are products of a psychopathic period. Boys and girls who came of voting age in 1935 were born in 1914. Their earliest memories are of mob murder and war hysteria. Their next, the cynical reaction to war's sentimentality and war's futility. Their adolescence was divided between the crass materialism of the jazz 1920's and the shock of the economic collapse. In effect, they went to high school in limousines and washed dishes in college.

Moreover, they had "seen instances too numerous to recite which they may conceivably interpret as a denial of all the traditions and principles in which Americans have been born and reared."[40] A typical example was the statement of a student at the University of Virginia: "We realize that honesty, integrity, and industry don't get you to the top any more. Our fathers had a lot of set rules for success. We know the world doesn't play by them now."[41]

That skepticism obviously extended to decisions about marriage and family during the 1930s. Marriages, which had averaged around 1.2 million per year during the 1920s, plummeted to 982,000 in 1932, before recovering dramatically to 1.3 million in 1934, after which they continued to rise. If couples were willing to marry by the mid-1930s, however, they continued to show a reluctance to have children. The birthrate had begun to decline in the late 1920s, and had fallen to 21.2 live births per thousand population by 1929. It remained above 20 during 1930 and 1931, then fell below 20 to stay throughout the remainder of the 1930s, reaching its bottom at 18.4 in 1933 and 1936, before surging above 20 again in 1941 (it remained above 20 until 1965). The result was that the size of the average family shrank more rapidly in the 1930s than in any previous decade.

SEX

A logical result of the postponement of marriage for many couples was an increase in premarital sex. One study among college juniors and seniors found that half the men and one-fourth of the women had experienced sexual intercourse.[42] The automobile, especially, provided "an incredible engine" for escape from parental supervision. As Bromley and Britten observed:

Boys today do not make formal calls on girls, nor pull candy in the kitchen, nor sit in a corner of the living-room and play the game of hearts under the critical eye of young brother. They honk the horn—most of them do not even bother to get out of the car and ring the doorbell—the girl comes running down the steps and they're off and away, out of reach of parental control.

And boys, they noted, were taking "full advantage of it, not only as a means of going places, but as a place to go where he can take his girl and hold hands, neck, pet, or, if it's that kind of an affair, go the limit." For those without access to an automobile the movies offered almost as much escape, and with the addition of sensual stimulation. Movies had, Bromley and Britten noted, "taken off the bedroom doors for young people and turned life into a French peep-show."[43]

Despite the increase of sexual activity among school-age Americans and a more liberal mood than had prevailed before World War I, most students were still deprived of adequate information on the subject in school. Even in college, students found that the closest many of their schools came to the subject of sex was classes on marriage and family, which generally skirted the information that students wanted most to have. There was too much emphasis on the future, and not enough on the "technical" matters of sex that students needed in their daily lives. Students in most colleges were learning nothing about contraception or the prevention and symptoms of venereal disease.[44]

In addition, it was estimated in the mid-1930s that somewhere between 750,000 and 1 million abortions were being performed annually in the United States, meaning that perhaps as much as one-third of the potential birth rate was being lost through abortion.[45] In a survey of 1,364 students on 46 college and university campuses, two-thirds were found to have known or heard of girls in their high schools who had undergone abortions.[46] Statistics could not, of course, be maintained on deaths from this illegal procedure, but authorities estimated that between 8,000 and 10,000 women died from abortions each year in the 1930s.[47]

Contraception had become more acceptable during the 1930s, although, as noted, students were learning little about it in school. "Planning" became a buzzword of the depression years, and it was given greater standing by the ballyhoo that surrounded the early New Deal's comic forays into what was hailed as economic planning. The buzzword was now extended to contraception, and "birth control" was now given the more respectable-sounding "scientific" title of "planned parenthood" or "family planning." Most young people, however, still learned about contraception from their friends and from pamphlets picked up in drugstores and gasoline stations that sold them. In her interviews with thousands of young people from coast to coast, Maxine Davis found that none of them had been "enlightened or in any way equipped to meet this situation by their parents, or by their family physician. Nor had any of them ever visited one of the few birth-control clinics."[48]

Contraceptives were widely available. Some college restrooms marketed condoms for a quarter through vending machines. They were also available through gasoline stations, tobacco stores, confectionaries, groceries, dry-good stores, and pool rooms, which, combined, were selling more condoms in the 1930s than the traditional supplier, the drugstores. One study estimated that the 15 chief manufacturers were producing 1.5 million condoms per day, with sales of approximately $25 million per year for the industry. At their cheapest, condoms were available for $1 per dozen. Estimates of total contraceptive sales varied from $125 million to $250 million per year.[49] This industry, at least, did not appear to be suffering from the depression.

In polls by *Country Home* magazine in 1930 and by *The Ladies' Home Journal* in 1938, American women responded overwhelmingly in favor of birth control, showing that it had strong support in both rural and urban America. Further evidence of support came from a poll of subscribers to the Protestant magazine *Churchman* in January 1935, and Gallup and

Fortune polls in 1936. In 1936 a U.S. Court of Appeals decision liberalized the conditions under which physicians could advise patients concerning contraception, and a resolution of the American Medical Association's annual convention in 1937 officially acknowledged birth control as a legitimate branch of medical practice. By 1938 there were more than 400 birth-control centers in the United States, located in every state in the union, and a scientific journal, *The Journal of Contraception*, was being published.[50]

The growing use of contraception naturally led to condemnation of the practice by the Catholic Church, particularly of the new rationale for its use. Where once its proponents had advocated it in Malthusian terms (a burgeoning population would outstrip the world supply of food), contraception was now frankly being advocated, one wrote, "to make the world safe for fornication."[51] Bromley and Britten found, however, that few college students (only 6 percent of their sampling) were allowing religion to influence their code of conduct.[52] And even the Catholic Church made limited concessions to the birth-control movement in the 1930s. In his encyclical, "Christian Marriage," Pope Pius XI in 1931 gave the Church's blessing to the so-called rhythm method of birth control, and American Catholics searched the bookstores for volumes on the Ohino-Knaus ("O.K.") cycle.[53]

The reduced number of births naturally led to a higher median age of the American population during the 1930s, when it jumped from 26.5 in 1930 to 29.0 by the end of the decade. By 1938 there were approximately 1.6 million fewer children under ten years of age than there had been in 1933. At the same time, maternal mortality rates fell by one-fourth between 1934 and 1938.

YOUTH AND THE DEPRESSION

Most youths, especially, faced a bleak future for the duration of the depression, at least. On average they were forced to wait two years between leaving school and finding employment. In 1935 an estimated 4.2 million youth were seeking work, and in 1940 the census concluded that "youth have suffered more unemployment than any other element of the labor force."[54] "Back to School" drives in 1931 and 1932 encouraged young people to continue their education rather than sit idle. In 1937 the number of high school graduates was nearly double the 1929 figure.[55] Others took to the road, some of them "riding the rails," in search of work rather than staying home where they would be a burden on their families. Many joined the Civilian Conservation Corps (CCC) after it was established by the Roosevelt administration in 1933. The CCC reached a peak enrollment of nearly a half million in 1935, most of them in their teens, of whom about 10 percent were blacks.[56]

Another New Deal youth agency was the National Youth Administration (NYA), organized in June of 1935, and open to both boys and girls. At its peak in 1937, the NYA numbered over 600,000 recipients in its two major programs, most of whom were receiving financial assistance to attend either high school or college. To earn their assistance, students worked at such tasks as mending and cataloging library books. Some conservative oldsters, Dixon Wecter pointed out, were disappointed in "a generation of hitchhikers, seeking to thumb a ride from Uncle Sam."[57] All told it was estimated by mid-1939 that the CCC and NYA combined had aided nearly 5 million young persons, with the number about evenly split between the two agencies, but approximately 4 million youths still remained unemployed.[58]

The bleak economic situation of the 1930s, combined no doubt with the New Deal's orientation toward class divisions and conflict, led many youths to become involved in organizations like the American Youth Congress and other, even more radical, groups such as the Student League for Industrial Democracy and the National Student League (later merged into the American Student Union in 1935), both of which tended to follow the line prescribed by Moscow. Concern about what was being taught to college students led many states to require loyalty oaths from teachers and professors in the 1930s.[59]

Most of America's youth, however, clearly wanted nothing more than to find employment, get married, and begin raising a family, the preoccupations of most youth even during the celebrated "roaring twenties," despite the publicity given to the relatively few in that decade who practiced "free love," experimented with drugs and perversion at "wild parties," and rejected conventions. Boys and girls, alike, however, found dating, courtship, and marriage much more difficult in depression times than during the boom. Money was needed by boys who wanted to take girls on dates, boys and girls alike needed respectable clothes to go "out," and girls needed the means for required make-up and hair care. If these difficulties were surmounted, it was still a long way to the economic security required for marriage. But biological necessities could not be denied, and a 1937 survey found that one-half of the college men and one-fourth of the college women responding had experienced premarital intercourse. A survey the previous year found three out of five college girls and half the men expressing a desire to wed soon after graduation. By 1938, however, it was estimated that about 1.5 million young people had been forced to postpone marriage, with many of them still living under their parents' roof.[60]

RELIGION AND ITS SUBSTITUTES

One might expect that the difficulties of the depression years, and particularly the crisis over values and standards, would cause many

Americans to seek comfort and guidance in the nation's churches or perhaps in new sects designed to meet the needs of the 1930s. This did not, however, happen. Although the 1930s did see the emergence of several new sects—most notably those of the black evangelist Father Divine in Harlem, who was hailed by his followers as God; and the Great I Am and Mankind United movements in California—and the growing popularity of others, particularly the Jehovah's Witnesses, there was no mass movement back to religion. In fact, if anything the reverse occurred. One study reports that during the 1930s nearly 3 million members were lost by the nation's churches, and a 1939 Gallup Poll found that half the people surveyed were attending worship services less often than their parents, while only about one-fifth exceeded their parents. Youth, especially, seemed to find little in organized religion that was relevant to their lives in the 1930s.[61] Sundays, as noted earlier, had become for most people an opportunity for excursions in the family automobile and its evenings the occasion for the family to gather before the radio for their favorite programs.

Yet, as Frederick Lewis Allen observed, organized religion faced other competition during the 1930s for the type of idealism that normally brought people to the churches. That competition was the sectarian social-mindedness of the New Deal years, in large part fomented by President Roosevelt, himself, beginning with his inaugural address. While the New Deal was the most important and popular of these movements for "salvation" of one type or another, it quickly spawned formidable competitors in Upton Sinclair's, "EPIC," Huey Long's "Share-Our Wealth" (SOW), the Townsend Plan, Father Coughlin, and, less importantly, the communists and others. These "religions of social salvation," as Allen calls them, gained their maximum support in the two or three years after the end of the New Deal "honeymoon."[62]

CHAPTER EIGHT

Coping

THE FAMILY BUDGET

The 1930s posed unusual challenges for housewives. Unemployment or underemployment of the breadwinner created new stresses for the family, not the least of which was finding food for the table while making all other budgetary ends meet. A National Resources Committee study reported that during 1935–36 there were 39 million consumer units—families or individuals—whose annual incomes averaged approximately $1,500. Two-thirds received less than that amount, while one-third got less than $780. One in thirty earned $5,000 or more. Of approximately $50 billion available for consumer spending, Americans spent $17 billion on food, $9.5 billion on housing, $5.25 billion on clothing, $5.3 billion on household operation, $3.8 billion on automobiles, $1.6 billion on recreation, and about $1.5 billion on household furnishings and equipment. Tobacco, which soothed nerves and dulled hunger pangs, took nearly twice as much from consumer pocketbooks as either books or education.[1]

Farmers had already experienced a depression from the early 1920s onward. That was bad news for farmers and their families but good news for urban consumers, because it meant low food prices at their neighborhood markets. When the depression spread to the rest of America beginning with 1930, the shock was somewhat cushioned because the price of food, already low, fell even further. But unemployment or reduced hours of work meant that a growing number of families were forced to look for ways to feed themselves at even less cost, without sacrificing essential nutrients. By 1933 an estimated one-fourth of Americans were

123

out of work—nearly 13 million workers and their families, representing perhaps 30–40 million adults and children.

When Franklin Delano Roosevelt assumed the presidency in March 1933, he instituted the New Deal, which brought federal relief payments to destitute Americans but also higher food prices. The Agricultural Adjustment Administration tried to solve the problems of farmers by reducing the amount they produced. With "surplus" production eliminated, the reduced supply should bring the farmers higher prices for their goods. Farmers were compensated for reducing their production by a tax levied on processors of agricultural goods (meat packers, flour mills, etc.) by the federal government that was paid to them. Naturally, food processors passed the cost of the tax on to consumers by adding it to the price of the meat, bread, and other foods that they processed. Consumers, therefore, found their food bills increased by the New Deal in two ways: by the reduction in supplies and by the addition of the tax.

In 1933, while many Americans were destitute and hungry, the federal government slaughtered pigs before they could grow to market size and mandated the plowing up of fields before they were ready to harvest. It was a curious spectacle, with food being destroyed in the midst of hunger. As if to show the folly of such thoughtlessness, Mother Nature now produced a disastrous drought that reduced American food supplies even further. The combination of human foolishness and nature reduced supplies of some foods by as much as 50 percent, driving up prices more, and one of the leading food exporters in the world was now forced to *import* food to feed its own people.

Meanwhile, states and municipalities had experienced falling revenues during the depression years owing to property tax delinquency and other reasons. Faced with the difficulty, indeed often the impossibility, of meeting payrolls and providing basic services, many turned to new forms of taxation in order to restore their treasuries to health. One incentive for them to do so was provided by the federal government that, under the Roosevelt administration, dangled the prospect of federal money for various desirable projects if the states provided "matching funds." Taxes on goods entering a state from another state became common, while state income taxes multiplied until about two-thirds of the states had some form of this tax by the end of the decade. A relatively new innovation was the sales tax, adopted by both states and municipalities during the 1930s, which 21 states had enacted by 1935 despite its regressive nature. The repeal of prohibition also offered potential revenue for the states, and 15 of them made the selling of liquor a state monopoly, while others imposed taxes on its sale. To rising prices, then, there was added the burden of higher taxation.

The result was that beginning with the winter of 1933–34 Americans were caught in a double squeeze: forced to confront not only reduced incomes but also much higher food prices. Various agencies of the federal government, state governments, universities and colleges, newspapers and household magazines, all began to devote attention to the problem of providing nutritional meals for families living on the margin of survival by providing shopping advice and menus.

COPING IN THE KITCHEN

Magazines during the depression years told cooks how to prepare canned meats, such as chickens, hams, sausage, tongue, corned beef, beef hash, and veal loaf. Since the canned meats had already been cooked in the canning process, preparation time was shorter and fuel was saved. Other items could be baked with them in the oven for the same time and at the same temperature. Canned chickens could be roasted, fried, fricasseed, or broiled, with delicious sauces and gravies made from the juices of the can.

Housewives were told that canned foods were teeming with vitamins and other nutritional needs, and were just waiting for the imaginative cook to produce culinary triumphs from them. A humble can of baked beans, for example, could be placed in a 400 ° oven for 30 minutes with a blanket of tiny sausages (pork or frankfurter)—fresh or from the can—and when served with canned brown bread it could produce a satisfying dinner dish that would be appreciated by the whole family. A can of green peas could be combined with a can of cream of mushroom soup and a tablespoon of minced parsley, poured into a baking dish and topped with finely cut American cheese or crumbs dotted with shortening. After 10 minutes in a 400 ° oven the housewife could serve a pleasing luncheon fit for the most discriminating guests.

Canned vegetables, housewives were told, could be enhanced by simple additions like a bit of simmered minced red and green pepper served atop heated green beans, or a bit of minced fresh mint and butter heated with canned peas. Canned tomatoes could be made more appealing for a family by serving them in individual ramekins, topped with chopped salted nuts, buttered croutons, a teaspoon of green peas, or even buttered popcorn if there were children in the house. A tablespoon of sugar to each three cups of pulp improved the flavor of tomatoes, and canned tomatoes were also good escalloped with a little tapioca added as a thickener before baking.

Some typical depression recipes using canned foods follow.

Canned Beef Stew Surprise

2 cans of beef stew
1 medium onion chopped
Chili sauce to taste
Flour to thicken gravy

Separate the meat from the potatoes. Drain the latter well, combine with chopped onions, brown the mixture in hot drippings, and the result is a nice dish of hashed-browns. The meat, gravy, and vegetables go into a pan with a good dose of chili sauce stirred in. Thicken the gravy with flour, put it all on the table with a tomato and lettuce salad.

Salami Scallop

6 slices salami

3 cups canned sweet corn

2 cups white sauce

1 pimiento

½ cup buttered bread crumbs

Cut sliced salami in half. Mix corn with seasoned white sauce and chopped pimiento. [Make white sauce by melting ¼ cup butter, adding ¼ cup of flour, and stirring in 2 cups of milk. When thickened, season to taste with salt and pepper.] In a casserole arrange layers of corn mixture and half slices of salami placed to overlap each other around the dish. Top with buttered bread crumbs and bake for 30 minutes in a 350° F. oven.

Salmon Chops

1 cup flaked salmon (one tall can)

1 cup dry bread crumbs

¼ teaspoon prepared mustard

1 tablespoon lemon juice

1 ½ cups thick white sauce

1 egg

Mix the salmon, ½ cup bread crumbs, mustard, lemon juice, and white sauce. Place mixture in refrigerator to cool and set. Shape like chops. Insert a short length of uncooked macaroni for the chop bone. Coat with egg and remaining crumbs and fry until crisp and brown. If using deep fat, the temperature should be 390° F.

Tuna and Potato Casserole

1 large can of tuna

3 or 4 potatoes, sliced thin

3 or 4 stalks of celery, chopped coarsely

1 large bunch of carrots, sliced thin

2 cups white sauce

½ cup bread crumbs

Arrange layers of tuna, potatoes, celery, and carrots in a baking dish and pour over all the well-seasoned white sauce. Cover with fine bread crumbs and bake in a moderate oven.

Potato-Kidney Bean Loaf

2 cups cooked or canned kidney beans

½ cup milk

3 tablespoons butter or meat drippings

¾ teaspoon salt

3 cups hot riced potatoes

½ cup milk

½ teaspoon salt

1 teaspoon butter

Pepper to taste

Press beans through sieve or ricer and blend with the milk, butter or drippings, and salt. Place in a greased baking dish and cover with potatoes, which have been blended with the remaining ingredients. Brown in a 400 ° F. oven and serve with a spicy tomato sauce.

Faced with reduced incomes and inflated food prices during the New Deal years, housewives found the high cost of meat the most difficult hurdle to surmount in planning meals. Two obvious solutions were to reduce the amount of meat in the family diet, or to buy cheaper cuts. Both courses of action were strongly recommended by nutritionists during the 1930s.

The food budget of the average American family in normal times found 30–40 percent spent on meat, poultry, and fish; with another 25 percent spent on eggs, dairy products, and fats. Breadstuffs and other grain products accounted for only 15–20 percent and vegetables and fruits only 15 percent. Nutritionists promised substantial reductions would occur in the family food budget if only those percentages were altered. Ideally, food money should be divided into fifths, with approximately 20 percent spent on each of the groups: vegetables and fruits; milk and cheese; breads and cereals; fats, sugar, etc.; and meats, fish, and eggs. The result would not only be a savings of money but also a healthier diet for the family.

For many families, however, such a redistribution of the food budget was not enough. Government agencies, magazines, and newspapers recognized that many households could barely afford proper nutrition. Government agencies, which dealt directly with families on welfare, devoted more attention than the others to the "below average" food budget, and some newspapers also addressed the problem by providing low-cost menus in their pages. Magazines for homemakers occasionally offered suggestions but were for the most part concerned with the "average" food budget, perhaps on the sensible theory that those who could not afford adequate nutrition were not likely to be magazine purchasers.

For those households with a below-average food budget, grains were likely to be the principal source of protein, with meats, fish, eggs, and poultry in the category of luxuries. Yet nutritionists warned that grains alone were not an adequate source of protein. Meat was an essential in the diet of the most impoverished household, even if in reduced amounts. To meet the problem, nutritionists encouraged the use of cheaper cuts of meat so that families could have meat at least once a day, three or four days a week. Cheap meats were not necessarily of poorer grade than the more expensive ones, housewives were told, and might actually be more nutritious. The high prices charged for some meats were, after all, largely a matter of "fashion," they pointed out, as witness the higher price that liver commanded once its effect on anemia was discovered.

Both the average and below-average food budgets, then, could benefit from the purchase of cheaper cuts of meat, although for the latter they were a lifesaver. Cooks were encouraged to experiment in substituting cheaper cuts of meat in their existing recipes or to use cheaper meats as extenders. Shoulder of lamb, for example, was suggested as a substitute for leg of lamb, beef liver for calves' liver, beef stew instead of steak. Boned shoulder of lamb and loin of veal were recommended as substitutes for beef in many dishes. Braised ox joints were also suggested as a cheap and delicious meat dish. Veal was so cheap in the 1930s that its use was encouraged even as an extender for chicken.

The preparation of cheaper meats, however, presented problems. For one, they generally required much longer cooking time in order to extract the flavor from the bones and to soften the connective tissues to make them tender enough for the table. For another, the longer cooking time frequently deprived the meat of much of its flavor. The latter problem could be overcome through the addition of herbs and spices, or bouillion or onion soup during cooking, or by cooking the meat together with other foods that would add flavor to it—vegetables, dressings, etc.

The longer cooking that was required, however, presented another problem for depression-era housewives. Time was not the problem, since householders typically had more of it than money during the depression. The difficulty was the fuel required for the longer cooking, the cost of which could eat up much of the money saved by purchasing the cheaper meat. Fuel was not so cheap that it could be taken for granted. Newspaper stories were common in the 1930s of people arrested for illegally reattaching gas and electric lines after their service had been cut off for delinquent payments. On wintry days, libraries and other warm buildings attracted large numbers of people who could not afford to heat their homes adequately.

Ingenuity was required, then, to find methods of cooking cheaper meats that would not eat up too much of the fuel budget. To tenderize cheaper cuts of meat and thus shorten the cooking time somewhat, cooks were advised to: 1) score the meat with a knife or special meat scorer; 2) put it through a meat grinder; or 3) alone or in combination with #1, marinate it in an acid solution such as vinegar water, cider, tomato juice, or French dressing. Of course, cooks were also encouraged to stew or braise the cheaper cuts (moist heat) in order to make them into tender dishes, and to use lower cooking temperatures in the oven and on top of the stove, whichever was used.

Braising was highly recommended. It consists of browning the meat in fat, then cooking it slowly in a covered dish with water and vegetables for flavor, after which the resulting juices are used to make thick brown gravy. Fuel was conserved since the cooking temperature was kept below the boiling point during the long cooking period, and the meat and vegetables for the meal were both cooked over the same burner or at the same time in the oven.

Cooks were also encouraged to be innovative in using the cheaper cuts in stews, hashes, and ragouts, to add variety to menus and permit their imaginations and creative abilities to have full play. The essential factor for perfection in such cooking was the blending of several flavors rather than merely using salt and pepper—a few peppercorns, for example, or a bit of bay leaf, a few sprigs of parsley, sometimes a pinch of thyme or some cloves stuck in an onion, or some mustard rubbed on the surface of the uncooked meat, perhaps a teaspoon of tarragon vinegar or a little cooking or regular wine, a dash of sage with pork, or chili powder, ketchup, or Worcestershire sauce with beef or lamb. Through such creativity a cook could ensure that no two stews would be exactly alike. An investment in 50 cents worth of seasonings, cooks were told, would provide months of cooking adventures.

Cooks were also advised, when stewing or braising cheap cuts of meat, to sear the meat in seasoned shortening (shortening to which garlic, minced onion, or perhaps carrot had been added) before adding the hot water or stock. Cold water should not be poured over meat since it would draw out all the flavor and leave stringy, flat-tasting meat. Timing was important when adding vegetables to meat dishes. If they were to flavor the meat, they should be added early, but if they were to retain their individuality, they should be added late and given just enough time to cook. A tablespoon of evaporated milk added just before serving would add gloss and richness.

Cooks were also advised not to open the oven door or lift the cover of the pan during cooking, since each such action released heat and used up precious fuel. Once a kettle began to boil, the heat should be turned down, since the food would cook just as fast on lower heat and with much less use of fuel. Electric stoves could be turned off altogether during the last ten minutes of cooking. Pans should be only large enough for the food being cooked, with no waste space, and covers should fit snugly.

When possible, entire meals should be cooked on a single heating unit, using double or triple pans or combining foods together in one. The same was true of oven use. Meals could be planned in combinations that would cook for similar times and at similar temperatures; those requiring shorter times could be inserted later. At a minimum, several foods should be cooked with one preheating of the oven—including bread and cakes, in addition to the food for the meal—with adjustments of the temperature as necessary. As a result, one-dish meals featuring cheaper cuts of meat became popular items in the menus of both average and below-average household budgets, whether cooked on the range or in the oven.

The recipes that follow offer samples of the cheaper cuts of meat that were used during the Great Depression and the imaginative ways in which they were prepared to both enhance their taste appeal and conserve fuel.

Fake Steak

1 ½ pounds ground beef

½ pound ground pork, with some fat

1 egg, beaten slightly

½ cup fine cracker or bread crumbs

Salt and pepper to taste

Mix the beef and pork, then add the beaten egg, crumbs, and seasoning. One-half cup milk may be added to the mixture if you desire a very moist product. Shape on an ovenproof platter to resemble porterhouse steak. Place in a preheated broiler with the top of the meat about 3 inches below the element or flame. Broil until nicely browned, turn and brown again. Arrange alternate halves of tomatoes and Bermuda onions around the meat (onions should be parboiled until almost tender). Dot each half with shortening and sprinkle with salt and sugar. Return to the broiler and continue cooking until vegetables are tender. Sprinkle the tomatoes with a little grated cheese and serve from the oven platter. Serves 6.

Liver Stew

1 pound of beef liver, cubed

2 tablespoons bacon fat

2 cups water

3 tablespoons flour

½ teaspoon salt

1/8 teaspoon pepper

½ teaspoon gravy seasoning

2 bunches carrots, scraped, sliced, and cooked

5 medium-sized potatoes, pared, quartered, and cooked

Sauté liver in bacon fat until brown, add water and cook 20 minutes or until tender. Thicken gravy with flour, then add salt, pepper, gravy seasoning, carrots, and potatoes. Simmer three minutes more.

Liverburgers

1 pound sliced beef liver

½ medium onion, sliced

½ cup cooked rice

1 egg

½ teaspoon dry mustard

1 teaspoon salt

¼ teaspoon pepper

1 tablespoon Sherry

Sauté the liver in butter or bacon fat, then put through grinder with the sliced onion. Mix with remaining ingredients, adding the Sherry last, and stir thoroughly. Fry in butter or bacon fat for 10 minutes, or until well browned, and serve on onion rolls.

Porcupine Ham Balls

1 pound cured ham shank, ground

½ pound fresh lean pork, ground

½ cup uncooked rice

½ teaspoon brown sugar

2 tablespoons shortening

No. 2 can cream of tomato soup or canned tomatoes

Combine the meat, rice, and brown sugar, mold into balls, and brown carefully in the shortening. Place in a baking dish and cover with the tomato soup or canned tomatoes. [If canned tomatoes are used, season with 1 bay leaf, 1 tablespoon chopped onion, 1 tablespoon chopped celery, 1 tablespoon brown sugar, and 1 teaspoon chopped red pepper.] Cover and bake in a moderate oven (325° to 350° F.) for 1 hour. The sauce may be thickened with 1 tablespoon of flour, if desired. Serve the sauce over the meat balls.

Breaded Lamb Neck Slices

6 lamb neck slices, one inch thick

Salt and pepper to taste

1 egg, beaten

2 tablespoons cold water

Crushed corn flakes or rice flakes

¼ cup bacon fat

1 cup hot water, meat stock, or thin tomato juice

Sprinkle the neck slices with salt and pepper and dip in the combined egg and cold water. Roll in the crushed flakes and brown, turning once, in the bacon fat. Add the hot water, stock, or tomato juice. Cover and simmer on top of the stove (or bake in a slow oven at 325° F.) for 1 hour, or until very tender. If any liquid remains, remove the cover and cook until it has evaporated and the lamb slices are brown. Served with sauteed pears and mint jelly.

Housewives in the 1930s made extensive use of white sauces to make foods filling, and to add calories and flavor at low cost. Other extenders were also used, including potatoes, kidney beans, and pasta, as well as gravies, stuffing, rice, and tapioca. Crumbs—both cracker and bread—were also used extensively as fillers. Egg noodles, for example, added to a little beef broth or chicken stock grew to a sizable serving due to the swelling of the noodles. In the same way Chinese noodles were used to extend creamed dishes. Crackers, too, were a cheap way to satisfy hunger, and were often used for children's school lunches. Some typical recipes using extenders follow.

Cracker-Stuffed Cabbage

1 medium-sized head of cabbage

2 tablespoons butter

½ teaspoon salt

12 crackers

Hot milk

4 eggs, beaten

1 small onion, minced fine

1 tablespoon butter

Salt and pepper to taste

Pull off and save the large outside leaves of cabbage and cut the inside leaves in shreds. Cook the shredded leaves with very little water until tender, for about 10 minutes, and add 2 tablespoons of butter and salt. Roll 12 crackers and moisten with enough hot milk to make a stiff paste. Add eggs, the onion sauteed in a tablespoonful of butter until soft, the cooked cabbage, salt and pepper, and mix all thoroughly. Lay a thin piece of muslin cloth in a deep dish, place the large leaves in this, giving them the shape of a cabbage, and fill with the mixture. Draw the cloth tightly together over this and tie. Place in a 4-quart pot of boiling water to which 1 tablespoon of salt has been added. Boil for 30 minutes. Remove the cloth and slice. Serve very hot with melted butter.

Kidney Bean Casserole

½ cup chopped raw or cooked meat

2 cups boiled or canned kidney beans

3 medium carrots, cut fine

1 medium onion, cut fine

1 cup canned or fresh tomatoes

½ cup milk

Salt, pepper, celery salt to taste

Brown the meat in a small amount of fat and combine with other ingredients. Season with salt, pepper, and celery salt. Place in a buttered baking dish, cover, and bake at 350° F. for 45 minutes or until vegetables are tender.

Corn Pudding with Bacon

4 strips of bacon

½ teaspoon of salt

¼ teaspoon of sugar

¼ cup of melted butter

1 cup of cracker crumbs

1 cup of milk

2 cups of corn

2 eggs

1 teaspoon of minced parsley

Fry the bacon until crisp and crumble into bits. Add the salt, sugar, and melted butter to the cracker crumbs. Add milk. Pour over canned corn and blend well. Add beaten eggs, minced bacon, and parsley. Pour into a shallow baking dish and bake in a slow oven.

Sauerkraut Casserole

1 quart sauerkraut

2 cups tomatoes

1 onion sliced

Pepper

One-half of a recipe for baking powder biscuits

Rinse kraut with cold water, combine with tomatoes, onion, and pepper, and simmer slowly for about 10 minutes. Place in a deep casserole or baking dish and cover with biscuit dough crust. Bake at 400° F. for 15 to 20 minutes, until the biscuit topping is puffed and brown.

Cheese Cutlets

2/3 cup grated cheese

2 cups mashed potatoes

4 tablespoons minced pimiento

1 cup cooked lima or navy beans, ground

1 teaspoon salt

Combine ingredients and shape the mixture into cutlets about one-half inch thick. Sauté them in a small amount of hot fat and serve with horseradish sauce.

Horseradish sauce

1 teaspoon mustard

3 tablespoons cream

1 tablespoon vinegar

Salt

Horseradish

Mix the first four ingredients and add as much horseradish as needed to make it the desired thickness.

Cottage Cheese Nut Loaf

1 cup cottage cheese

1 cup chopped pecans

1 cup bread crumbs

1 tablespoon lemon juice

½ teaspoon salt

Pinch of pepper

2 tablespoons chopped onion

1 tablespoon butter

Combine the cottage cheese, nuts, bread crumbs, lemon juice, salt and pepper. Mix with onion which has been cooked in butter and a little water until tender. Bake in a loaf pan in moderate oven until brown.

Spinach Casserole

6 medium-sized potatoes

3 eggs, beaten

¼ cup of butter or margarine

1 teaspoon salt

1 teaspoon pepper

1 pound spinach, washed and chopped very fine

Pare and then grate potatoes directly into well-beaten eggs to prevent discoloration. Add butter and salt and pepper. Place half of potato mixture in buttered casserole, pack in spinach, then top with remaining potato mixture. Bake in 350° F. oven for 2 hours or until potatoes are tender and well-browned on top.

Lima Bean Casserole

2 cups cooked lima beans

½ cup milk

½ cup cream

½ teaspoon salt

1 teaspoon sugar

¼ cup green pepper, chopped

¼ cup Spanish onion, chopped

2 tablespoons chopped pimiento

2 eggs, beaten

¼ teaspoon celery salt

Combine all ingredients and turn into a well-buttered casserole dish. Bake about 30 minutes in a moderate (350° F.) oven.

CONSUMER SPENDING

Concern about nutrition as a result of the depression, combined with advances made in the 1920s and 1930s in vitamin research, led Americans to begin to ingest large quantities of vitamin concentrates during the 1930s. By the winter of 1938–39 vitamins were reported to be second only to laxatives among products sold over the drug counter, and vitamin manufacturers reported themselves unable to keep up with the demand. Prepared foods began to be sold with vitamin enrichments in order to capitalize on the mania. Since the sale of beer lagged during the chilly winter months, one major brewery began to promote a new Sunshine Vitamin D Beer, the only beer that, because it contained sunshine vitamin D, was actually good for the imbiber during the winter months. The promotion of the new beer, was, however, quickly undermined by the competition, one major brewery proclaiming that its own beer was "undoctored and untreated," and "not a patent medicine."[2]

The high tide of electrical appliance sales, which had characterized the 1920s because of the greater availability of electricity, high-pressure advertising, and consumer credit, receded in the 1930s, except for the sale of electric refrigerators, which had come to be regarded as a necessity by then in most households. Other time- and labor-saving devices did not seem so important during the depression.

Cigarette production and consumption boomed in the 1930s, with the typical American male consuming between 1,000 and 1,200 per year, and some smoking as many as 10,000. Smoking by women, too, was commonplace by the 1930s. Americans also loved their coffee, and averaged four cups a day of it, as well as their candy, chewing gum, and soft drinks.[3] Dining out slackened in the early years of the depression despite reductions in restaurant prices. At the time of Roosevelt's inauguration in March 1933, the Ambassador Cafe in Omaha was offering a ten-course Sunday dinner for 60 cents, including a rose for the lady or a cigar for the gentleman.[4]

Many women extended the purchasing power of their shrinking clothing/fashion budgets in the early 1930s by making some of their own clothing. Many housewives similarly resurrected the long-abandoned arts of home soapmaking, bread baking, dry cleaning, pickling, and preserving. While sales of glass canning jars rose during the early 1930s, the sale of canned goods declined.

If Middletown can be taken as representative of America in general, it was expenditures on "luxuries" that declined most during the depression—things such as jewelry (the number of jewelry stores in Middletown dropped from ten to four and spending on jewelry fell 85 percent in value), candy, restaurant dining, and replacement of durable goods.[5]

FAMILIES AS ENTREPRENEURS

Curiously, despite a halving of retail dollar spending during the early years of the depression, there were actually 6 percent more retail establishments in Middletown in 1933 than in 1929. In part this was certainly the result of what the Lynds called "inventiveness," but what others might call desperation, of people seeking to replace the income lost due to the absence of employment. The Lynds wrote:

Little signs in yards announce the presence of household beauty parlors and cleaning and pressing businesses; grocery stores have been opened in cottage front rooms or in additions to residences built out flush with the street; some houses on prominent corners have installed on the corner of the lot little ice-cream and soft-drink booths in the form of spotless ice-cream freezers twelve feet high and eight feet in diameter; others have cashed in on the forced sales of old farms in this section of the state by opening household antique shops; while one woman whose husband's flourishing meat market went under is serving well-appointed dinners in her home to local women's clubs and sororities.[6]

Presumably this same entrepreneurial struggle for survival characterized people in other towns and cities of the nation as well, with small-scale business establishments, odd-job work, and barter—a considerable portion of which never found its way into economic statistics.

THE REVIVAL OF BACKYARDS AND GARDENING

One aspect of Middletown that struck the Lynds was the revival of backyards as places to spend leisure time, to socialize, and to pursue gardening. All of this represented a distinct change from 1925, and made the Middletown of 1935 seem to them closer to the 1880s than to the city they had studied only a decade earlier.[7] Gardening, however, was another way by which Americans coped with the depression, especially with the higher food prices caused by New Deal policies and natural calamities. Surplus garden produce was canned for use at other times of the year, and home and garden magazines featured numerous articles on gardening and home food preservation. Middletown's glass factory was one industry that suffered no ill-effects from the depression, for it manufactured the jars that were in high demand during the 1930s for home food preservation.[8]

Not everyone, of course, had a backyard suitable for food cultivation. Middletown joined most of the rest of the nation in providing free seed and vacant lots for the unemployed to grow food on. By the spring of 1933 at least 2,500 Middletonians were taking advantage of the opportunity.[9] The American Public Health Association's Committee on Foods reported in 1934 that "unemployment, reduced incomes, home and welfare garden projects have been instrumental in greatly stimulating home food preservation." State agricultural experiment stations and extension services, as well as welfare agencies, had sponsored Canning Club projects across the nation. In some cases communities had installed canning kitchens to conserve surplus food grown in both welfare and home gardens for use by those on relief. A Massachusetts study, it reported, had found that $1 spent on gardening and canning projects returned benefits equivalent to $2 spent on other methods of direct relief.[10]

Many states appointed gardening directors to coordinate relief gardening activities; gardening instructions were printed and distributed free of charge, as were seed and fertilizer; and some businesses, like International Harvester, also promoted gardens for laid-off employees in cities where they had plants. As early as 1933 the State of Indiana had provided 15,000 acres for welfare gardens. In Lakewood, New Jersey, 30,000 jars of canned vegetables were put up from surplus crops, 10,000 of which were allocated for relief recipients.[11]

SOCIALIZING

Although self-evident, one aspect of the depression years deserves emphasis: that all of the daily trials of families and individuals even in normal times—the bills that need paying, doctor and dentist visits, eye care, educational expenses, retirement planning, and many others—were more difficult and stress-producing during the 1930s. Even such normal activities as entertaining guests and being entertained, in turn, presented problems in the 1930s for families whose means were insufficient or whose situation was an embarrassment to them. Thus even the normal outlet of socialization was denied to many, especially during the early 1930s. And even those who had jobs were constantly haunted by the possibility that they might be thrown out of work in those uncertain times.

The unemployed, especially, found their social lives diminished, not only because of their poverty and their humiliation, but because they found that many of their erstwhile friends were of the "fair weather" variety. As an unemployed carpenter put it, "as soon as you are out of the dough, your friends don't want to know you any more. They are afraid you will ask them for something. People on relief are black sheep." An unemployed electrician agreed: "You don't have any friends unless you have got the dollar. If you have the dollar, you have got your true and loyal friend, and if you haven't got it, you're alone in the world." Another unemployed man said: "Our friends certainly did turn out to be fair-weather friends. Once they know you're down and out, they act as if you had a disease."[12]

A principal problem for the unemployed in socializing with employed friends was their inability to do things with them. Employed families wanted to go out, to take in a movie, perhaps go to a nightclub, but the unemployed could not afford it. Many dropped their church and club memberships because they could not afford money for the collection plate or for dues.[13] Children, too, were embarrassed by their condition and disliked going to school, where they were sometimes subjected to jibes. Adolescents, especially, found dating difficult under the circumstances, for lack of suitable clothing or the few dollars required to treat a date to a movie and refreshments.[14]

Conclusion

Historian Frederick Marks III has written that "the years spanning the New Deal must be described as belonging to an age of delayed adolescence, one which found a fitting symbol in FDR."[1] There is certainly much about the popular culture of the 1930s that deserves description as adolescent, even childish. Regression into an earlier, happier stage of life is, as we have seen, described by psychologists as a frequent method of escape from unpleasant realities. It is, perhaps, one explanation for much of the behavior during the 1930s that is otherwise so baffling.

Many observers of the popular culture of the 1930s linked aspects of it to psychological causes or came very near to doing so. We have seen in the preceding pages references to Americans seeking relief in "manic amusements" when in the "dumps"; to "staid people who want something else to think about" acting like little children; to people explaining their obsession with jigsaw puzzles because of their usefulness in escaping from thinking and worrying; to the "adult infantilism" of the 1930s; to the American desire to be "welded . . . into a safe mass"; to the popular literature of the 1930s as "a literature, not of inquiry, but of distraction," designed to take its readers "momentarily out of reality"; to the role of radio and the movies in assisting Americans "to escape monotonous, graceless reality," by transporting them "to a never-never land of adventure and romance uncomplicated by thought"; and many others.

Bernard DeVoto found similarities between the 1930s and the depressed 1840s. In both decades there was

a vacillation between rebellious, evangelical excitement and stunned apathy. Maladjustment and panic produced social pathology, as they always do. To-day has no novelties worth mentioning—most of its pathology you can find without effort in the fear-bound Forties. But the deepest of all was the malady of the mind that invariably accompanies social disaster.[2]

America, wrote another observer, was a manic-depressive case; when depressed, as in the 1930s, Americans sought manic amusements and happy endings.[3]

Clearly, the state of idleness caused by unemployment is not the same as the condition of having increased leisure time, nor are the consequences likely to be the same in both cases. Increased leisure time is usually a symbol of success, whereas the idleness of unemployment is exactly the opposite. Both require the filling of time, but unemployment is accompanied by blows to the ego that produce psychic challenges and responses, as well, which can profoundly affect the way in which the idle do so. Thus, while leisure and idleness may produce similar pastimes, and others that appear similar, the popular culture of a decade in which approximately 20 percent of the work force was unemployed must differ substantially from that of a decade in which only about 2 percent, on average, was idle.

This being the case, one striking aspect of the 1930s is certainly the vibrance of popular culture in absorbing the attention and energies of the American people during so traumatic a time. The depression lasted longer in the United States than anywhere else in the world and the experience was at least as shattering as elsewhere. Yet Americans marked time for an entire decade awaiting the economic recovery that was continually "just around the corner" according to their politicians. They watched a nascent recovery in 1936 crash in 1937 and 1938, and still they marked time. People in other lands were not so patient. Probably American popular culture deserves more credit than the nation's leaders and institutions for the patience shown in the United States. A nation busy jitterbugging has little time or energy left for political revolution.

At least one political leader of the 1930s recognized the role that popular culture could play in helping Americans to deal with the depression. In 1931, Gene Smith tells us, President Herbert Hoover observed that what America needed during those early years of the depression was "a great poem," something that would "lift people out of fear and selfishness."[4] Subsequently, Americans were gifted with a variety of "great poems" that served the need Hoover had described, from the songs of Walt Disney's Three Little Pigs and Seven Dwarfs, to the powerful works of Edna St. Vincent Millay, Stephen Benet, and Robert Frost. Roosevelt, too, by his reference, previously mentioned, to the effect of Shirley Temple's movies during the depression, clearly recognized the "soothing" effect that popular culture could exert during hard times. Hollywood's value as an "opiate" during the depression years can hardly be exaggerated, and yet it was only one aspect of the popular culture of the decade. Its contribution to American patience was fortified by those from the pulp magazines, radio, music, sports, and other elements of the popular culture.

The effects of popular culture also vitiated the appeals of demagogues of the left and right during the 1930s. The passionate rhetoric of the Huey Longs and Father Coughlins fell on ears that preferred the croonings of Rudy Vallee, the comic antics of Amos and Andy, and the triumphs over adversity of Shirley Temple. It was a decade when Americans looked for "star" qualities—not only in the movies, on the radio, and in sports, but even at marathon dances, walkathons, and in politics. The Longs, Coughlins, and Townsends could not attain star status.

One political figure was more successful. More than any president since his cousin Theodore, Franklin Delano Roosevelt became a part of the popular culture of his time through his radio presence and the drama and color of his presidency. It is certainly true, as Marks observed, that Roosevelt was "a fitting symbol" of the adolescence of the 1930s, but the president's own adolescent nature and behavior only increased his appeal among the people. Huey Long, Doctor Townsend, Father Coughlin, and all the rest were powerless against such star qualities for the 1930s, and so was Alf Landon. The congruence of Roosevelt's adolescent nature with that of the American people during the decade helps to explain his political success despite the failure of his policies and programs to bring economic recovery.

Americans coped. We might well wonder if in any such future crisis Americans will cope as well. Given the changes in our society since the 1930s, can popular culture ever again exert such an influence as it did during the decade of the Great Depression?

Notes

INTRODUCTION

1. P. Eisenberg and P. F. Lazarsfeld, "The Psychological Effects of Unemployment," *Psychological Bulletin*, 35 (1938), 378.

2. In Norman T. Feather, *The Psychological Impact of Unemployment* (New York: Springer-Verlag, 1990), p. 229.

3. John Hayes and Peter Nutman, *Understanding the Unemployed: The Psychological Effects of Unemployment* (London: Tavistock, 1981), pp. 22–23.

4. Peter Kelvin and Joanna E. Jarrett, *Unemployment: Its Social Psychological Effects* (New York: Cambridge University Press, 1985), pp. 60–61.

5. Charles Zastrow and Karen Kirst-Ashman, *Understanding Human Behavior and the Social Environment* (Chicago: Nelson-Hall, 1987), pp. 374–75.

6. I have found H. P. Laughlin, *The Ego and Its Defenses* (New York: J. Aronson, 1979), to be of particular value in its description of the multitude of ego defense mechanisms.

7. Ribot quoted in Clemens J. France, "The Gambling Influence," in John Halliday and Peter Fuller, eds., *The Psychology of Gambling* (New York: Harper & Row, 1974), pp. 127–28.

8. Lazarus in ibid., p. 128.

9. Wundt in ibid., p. 129.

10. Edmund Bergler, "The Psychology of Gambling," in ibid., p. 181.

11. Washington *Post*, 1–12–1936.

CHAPTER ONE

1. Foster R. Dulles, *America Learns to Play* (New York: Appleton-Century, 1965), pp. 366–68.

2. Omaha *World-Herald*, 6–29–1933.

3. *The Saturday Evening Post*, 6–24–1933, p. 20.

4. Bruce Bliven, "Worshipping the American Hero," in Fred J. Ringel, ed., *America as Americans See It* (New York: Harcourt, Brace, 1932), p. 129.

5. Will Payne, "The New Prohibition," *Saturday Evening Post*, 8–19–1933, pp. 23, 66.

6. *Commercial and Financial Chronicle*, 7–8–1939, p. 152.

7. Will Rogers to Daniel Roper, 12–13–1933, in Daniel Roper, *Fifty Years of Public Life* (Durham, NC: Duke University Press, 1941), p. 286.

8. Mark Sullivan to Martin Geoffrey, 2–20–1933, Mark Sullivan Papers, Library of Congress.

9. C. B. Reeves, "Brief for the Bankers," *American Mercury*, 9–32, p. 20.

10. *The Economist*, 12–23–1933, p. 1220.

11. Professor Willford I. King, in New York *Herald-Tribune*, 3–11–1934.

12. John M. Blum, "The Public Image: Politics," in Robert E. Spiller and Eric Larrabee, eds., *American Perspectives* (Cambridge, MA: Harvard University Press, 1961), p. 151.

13. *Nation's Business*, 5–1934, p. 9.

14. *Nation's Business*, 7–1934, p. 7.

15. James L. McCamy, *Government Publicity: Its Practice in Federal Administration* (Chicago: University of Chicago Press, 1939), p. 228.

16. *The Saturday Evening Post*, 6–24–1933, p. 20.

17. Omaha *World-Herald*, 5–5–1933.

18. *Nation's Business*, 5–1934.

19. "Does the World Owe Me a Living?" *Scribner's Magazine*, 5–1934, p. 425.

20. George Sokolsky, "The Psychology of the New Deal," *Atlantic Monthly*, 3–1936, pp. 369–73.

21. New York *Times*, 2–19–1936.

22. Omaha *World-Herald*, 4–13–1933 and 4–19–1933.

23. For a discussion of the New Deal war against business and banking, see Gary Dean Best, *Pride, Prejudice and Politics: Roosevelt versus Recovery, 1933–1938* (New York: Praeger, 1991).

24. Pinchot to Freda Kirchway (*The Nation*), 4–16–1935, Amos Pinchot Papers, Library of Congress.

25. Pinchot to Narcissa Swift (*Polity*), 5–4–1933, in ibid.

26. Pinchot to Henry Moskowitz, 8–9–1935, in ibid.

27. Pinchot to Arthur Williams, 10–28–1936, in ibid.

28. Pinchot to Darwin J. Meserole, 12–8–1937, in ibid.

29. Pinchot to Henry Pratt Fairchild, 9–27–1934, in ibid.

30. Pinchot to Hans Cohrssen, 2–18–1937, in ibid.

31. Pinchot to George Foster Peabody, 8–9–1935, in ibid.

32. Harold E. Stearns, "The Intellectual Life," in Harold E. Stearns, ed., *America Now* (New York: Scribner's 1938), pp. 375–77.

33. Francis X. Talbot, S. J., "Catholicism in America," in ibid., p. 540.

34. Robert E. Spiller, "Literature and the Critics," in Spiller and Larrabee, *American Perspectives*, p. 55.

35. Joseph Wood Krutch, "The Theatre," in Stearns, *America Now*, p. 78.

36. Dixon Wecter, *The Age of the Great Depression, 1929–1941* (New York: Macmillan, 1948), p. 253.

37. Mirra Komarovsky, *The Unemployed Man and His Family* (New York: Dryden, 1940), p. 117.

38. Ibid., p. 129.

39. Ibid., pp. 118–21.

40. Ibid., p. 122.

41. Ruth S. Cavan and Katherine H. Ranck, *The Family and The Depression* (Chicago: University of Chicago Press, 1938), pp. 152–53.

42. Ibid., p. 160.

43. Maxine Davis, *The Lost Generation* (New York: Macmillan, 1936), p. 41.

44. Ibid., pp. 41–46.

45. Ibid., p. 51.

46. Ibid., pp. 52–53.

47. Ibid., pp. 95–97.

48. Ibid., p. 18.

49. Quoted in Omaha *World-Herald*, 1–19–1936.

50. Omaha *World Herald*, 1–22–1936.

51. Quoted in Frederick Lewis Allen, *Since Yesterday* (New York: Bantam Books, 1965), p. 119.

52. Charles R. Hearn, *The American Dream in the Great Depression* (Westport, CT: Greenwood, 1977), pp. 109–12.

53. Ibid., pp. 122–23.

54. New York *Times*, 12–17–1938.

55. Alice G. Marquis, *Hopes and Ashes* (New York: Free Press, 1986), p. 10.

56. Elmer Davis, "The American at Leisure," in Ringel, *America as Americans See It*, p. 207.

57. Walter B. Pitkin, "The American: How He Lives," in ibid., p. 203.

58. John Steinbeck, "I Remember the Thirties," in Don Congdon, ed., *The Thirties* (New York: Simon & Schuster, 1962), p. 23.

59. Lowell Thompson, "America's Day-Dream," *Saturday Review*, 11–13–1937, p. 16.

60. M. B. Levick, "Games and Puzzles Gain," New York *Times*, 4–14–1935.

CHAPTER TWO

1. M. B. Levick, "Games and Puzzles Gain," New York *Times*, 4–14–1935.

2. Marshall Sprague, "New Games for Indoors," New York *Times*, 11–29–1936.

3. Levick, 4–14–1935.

4. George H. Copeland, "The Country Is Off on a Jig-Saw Jag," New York *Times Magazine*, 2–12–1933.

5. *Forbes*, 2–1–1933, p. 10.

6. New York *Times*, 4–6–1933.

7. *Business Week*, 6–17–1933, p. 12.

8. Ibid.

9. *Forbes*, 6–1–1933, p. 8.

10. *Literary Digest*, 7–8–1933, p. 30.

11. Frederick Lewis Allen, *Since Yesterday* (New York: Bantam Books, 1965), p. 27.

12. *Literary Digest*, 8–9–1930, pp. 29–31.

13. Ibid., pp. 30–31, 34.

14. Paul Sann, *Fads, Follies and Delusions of the American People* (New York: Crown, 1967), pp. 76–77.

15. *Time*, 12–14–1936, p. 58.

16. K. Crichton, "Jam in the Saucer," *Collier's*, 2–23–1935, pp. 26, 50.

17. *Time*, 2–3–1936, p. 24.

18. Quentin Reynolds, "Round & Round," *Collier's*, 8–22–1936, p. 38.

19. "Dance Marathoners," *The Survey*, 2–1934, p. 54.

20. J. B. Kennedy, "Good-Night Lady: Marathon Dancing," *Collier's*, 7–23–1932, p. 28.

21. Ibid., pp. 28, 44.

22. Ibid., p. 44.

23. Sann, *Fads, Follies*, p. 57.

24. "Dance Marathoners," p. 53.

25. Meridel Le Sueur, "The Sleepwalkers," *The New Republic*, 2–2–1933, p. 313.

26. Ibid., p. 314.

27. "Brother, Can You Share a Dime?" *The New Republic*, 5–22–1935, p. 43.

28. Ibid.

29. *Literary Digest*, 3–6–1937, p. 36.

30. Quoted in Sann, *Fads, Follies*, p. 98.

31. Ibid.

32. Ibid., p. 100.

33. *Literary Digest*, 5–18–1935, p. 38.

34. "Brother, Can You Share a Dime?" p. 43.

35. "Sport in the Nickel Age," *Business Week*, 3–29–1933, p. 14.

36. Allen, *Since Yesterday*, p. 123.

37. Samuel Lubell, "Ten Billion Nickels," *The Saturday Evening Post*, 5–13–1939, p. 12.

38. Ibid., pp. 11, 38.

39. Ibid., p. 38.

40. Ibid.

41. Allen, *Since Yesterday*, p. 123.

42. *Literary Digest*, 5–9–1936, p. 34.

43. Ibid.

44. Allen, *Since Yesterday*, p. 122.

45. Quoted in Foster R. Dulles, *America Learns to Play* (New York: Appleton-Century, 1965), p. 375.

46. Ibid., p. 377.

47. *Time*, 2–3–1936, p. 68, and 2–10–1936, p. 44.

48. New York *Times*, 4–19–1936.

49. Dulles, *America Learns to Play*, pp. 378–80.

50. Allen, *Since Yesterday*, p. 26.

51. Sann, *Fads, Follies*, p. 157.

52. J.A.G. Rice, "Play's the Thing," *The Saturday Evening Post* 4–7–1934, p. 206.

53. New York *Times*, 3–29–1936; *Nation's Business*, 5–19–1936, p. 7; Omaha *World-Herald*, 4–2–1936.

54. Omaha *World-Herald*, 4–2–1936 and 5–11–1936.
55. New York *Times*, 4–2–1936.
56. *Literary Digest*, 9–12–1936, p. 10.
57. Levick, "Games and Puzzles."
58. "Camera Action," *Business Week*, 1–5–1935, p. 29.
59. *Scientific American*, 9–1932, p. 170.
60. *Scientific American*, 9–1935, p. 152.
61. "1,500,000 Dry Shavers . . .," *Fortune*, 5–1938, pp. 70, 136.
62. Ibid.
63. Ibid., pp. 136, 138.

CHAPTER THREE

1. *Saturday Review*, 9–16–1933, p. 108.
2. Gilbert Seldes, "American Humor," in Fred J. Ringel, ed., *America as Americans See It* (New York: Harcourt, Brace, 1932), pp. 342, 350–51.
3. Lowell Thompson, "America's Day-Dream," *Saturday Review*, 11–13–1937, p. 3.
4. "Hooverism in the Funnies," *The New Republic*, 7–11–1934, p. 234.
5. *The New Republic*, 9–18–1935, p. 147.
6. Ibid.; and *The Nation*, 10–23–1935, p. 454.
7. Robert Heide and John Gilman, *Dime-Store Dream Parade* (New York: Dutton, 1979), pp. 73–74.
8. Frank Luther Mott, *American Journalism* (New York: Macmillan, 1962), p. 695.
9. Ibid., p. 694.
10. Thompson, "Day-Dream," p. 3.
11. *Editor and Publisher*, 7–2–1938.
12. Robert Benchley, "The Newspaper 'Game,' " in Ringel, *America as Americans See It*, pp. 332–35.
13. Ray Barfield, "Big Little Books," in M. Thomas Inge, ed., *Handbook of American Popular Literature* (Westport, CT: Greenwood, 1988), pp. 25–27.
14. Heide and Gilman, *Dime-Store*, p. 76.
15. Bill Blackbeard, "Pulps and Dime Novels," in Inge, *Handbook*, pp. 231–36.
16. Ibid., p. 309.
17. Robert Cantwell, "The Magazines," in Harold E. Stearns, ed., *America Now* (New York: Scribner's, 1938), pp. 350–51.
18. Ibid., pp. 351–52.
19. Maxine Davis, *The Lost Generation* (New York: Macmillan, 1936), p. 139.
20. Theodore B. Peterson, *Magazines in the Twentieth Century* (Urbana: University of Illinois Press, 1956), pp. 285, 292–93.
21. Clifton Fadiman, "What Does America Read?" in Ringel, *America as Americans See It*, p. 76.
22. Peterson, *Magazines*, p. 376.
23. Ibid., pp. 298–302.
24. Fadiman, in Ringel, *America as Americans See It*, p. 76.
25. Peterson, *Magazines*, pp. 303–4.
26. Ibid., pp. 273–81, and 311–12.

27. Ibid., pp. 262–63, 268.

28. Cantwell, in Stearns, *America Now*, p. 353.

29. Peterson, *Magazines*, pp. 283, 288.

30. Ibid., pp. 304–6.

31. James P. Wood, *Magazines in the United States* (New York: Ronald, 1956), pp. 215–16.

32. Peterson, *Magazines*, pp. 354–55.

33. Elmer Davis, "The American at Leisure," in Ringel, *America as Americans See It*, pp. 210–11.

34. Cantwell, in Stearns, *America Now*, p. 350.

35. Ibid., 349.

36. Charles R. Hearn, *The American Dream in the Great Depression* (Westport, CT: Greenwood, 1977), p. 249.

37. Sullivan to Bernie [Baruch], 1–31–1934, Sullivan Papers, Library of Congress; see also Frank Kent, Baltimore *Sun*, 9–6–1934.

38. Bernard DeVoto to Thomas W. Lamont, 12–28–1936, Thomas W. Lamont Papers, Baker Library, Harvard University.

39. Cantwell, in Stearns, *America Now*, p. 352.

40. Fadiman, in Ringel, *America as Americans See It*, p. 76.

41. Cantwell, in Stearns, *America Now*, p. 352.

42. Wood, *Magazines in the United States*, p. 299.

43. Ibid., p. 154.

44. *American Mercury*, 11–1932, p. 38.

45. *America Mercury*, 3–1936, p. 257.

46. Ibid.

47. *American Mercury*, 3–1939, p. 260.

48. Washington *Post*, 4–29–1934.

49. Albert Jay Nock, "The Amazing Liberal Mind," *American Mercury*, 8–1938, p. 469.

50. *American Mercury*, 7–1938.

51. Emily S. Watts, *The Businessman in American Literature* (Athens: University of Georgia Press, 1982), pp. 90–94.

52. Ibid., pp. 94–97.

53. Ibid., pp. 99–102.

54. David Madden, "Introduction," in David Madden, ed., *Tough Guy Writers of the Thirties* (Carbondale: Southern Illinois University Press, 1968), pp. xv–xvii.

55. Ibid., pp. xxvii–xxix.

56. New York *Herald-Tribune*, 1–21–1934.

57. Hearn, *American Dream*, p. 58.

CHAPTER FOUR

1. Frank Luther Mott, *American Journalism* (New York: Macmillan, 1962), pp. 702–4.

2. For a more complete description of the relations between the press and the Roosevelt administration, see Gary Dean Best, *The Critical Press and the New Deal* (Westport, CT: Praeger, 1993).

3. John Cowles, "Journalism—Newspapers," in Harold E. Stearns, ed., *America Now* (New York: Scribner's, 1938), p. 371.

4. Louis Stark of the New York *Times*, quoted in Leo C. Rosten, *The Washington Correspondents* (New York: Harcourt, Brace, 1937), pp. 266–67; also see Arthur Krock, "Washington, D.C.," in Hanson W. Baldwin and Shepard Stone, eds., *We Saw it Happen* (New York: Simon & Schuster, 1938), p. 5.

5. New York *Times*, 11–25–1934.

6. William E. Berchtold, "Press Agents of the New Deal," *New Outlook*, 7–26–1934, p. 24.

7. Cabell Philips, "Autocrats of the Breakfast Table," in Cabell Philips, ed., *Dateline: Washington* (Garden City, NY: Doubleday, 1949), p. 176.

8. Don Wharton, "Commentators," *Today*, 5–30–1936, p. 22.

9. Frederick Lewis Allen, *Since Yesterday* (New York: Bantam Books, 1965), p. 44.

10. Vice Admiral Ross T. McIntire, *White House Physician* (New York: Putnam's 1946), p. 82.

11. Raymond Clapper, Washington *Post*, 8–26–1935.

12. For a fuller description of the polls and the 1936 campaign, see Gary Dean Best, *Pride, Prejudice and Politics* (New York: Praeger, 1991), pp. 124, 133–34, 136–37.

13. *Editor and Publisher*, 1–5–1935.

14. Mott, *American Journalism*, pp. 682–83.

15. Edwin Emery, *The Press and America* (Englewood Cliffs, NJ: Prentice-Hall, 1972), p. 647.

16. Benchley, in Fred J. Ringel, ed., *America as Americans See It* (New York: Harcourt, Brace, 1932), pp. 332–35.

17. Ibid., p. 339.

18. Dixon Wecter, *The Age of the Great Depression 1929–1941* (New York: Macmillan, 1948), pp. 245–46.

19. Malcom M. Willey and Stuart A. Rice, *Communication Agencies and Social Life* (New York: McGraw-Hill, 1933), p. 186.

20. *United States News*, 6–3–1933.

21. J. Fred McDonald, *Don't Touch That Dial: Radio Programming in American Life from 1920 to 1960* (Chicago: Nelson-Hall, 1979), p. 38.

22. New York *Herald-Tribune*, 3–16–1933.

23. Maxine Davis, *The Lost Generation* (New York: Macmillan, 1936), p. 134.

24. Robert S. Lynd and Helen M. Lynd, *Middletown in Transition* (New York: Harcourt, Brace, 1937), pp. 144, 436.

25. Washington *Post*, 5–7–1937.

26. Louis R. Reid, "Amusement: Radio and Movies," in Stearns, *America Now*, p. 17.

27. Arthur F. Wertheim, *Radio Comedy* (New York: Oxford University Press, 1979), p. 46.

28. Deems Taylor, "Music," in Stearns, *America Now*, pp. 63–64.

29. Lynds, *Middletown in Transition*, p. 263.

30. Fortune, 1–1938, p. 91.

31. Alice G. Marquis, *Hopes and Ashes* (New York: Free Press, 1986), p. 47.

32. Wertheim, *Radio Comedy*, pp. 48, 113.
33. Bliven, in Ringel, *America as Americans See It*, p. 125.
34. Ibid., p. 113.
35. Wertheim, *Radio Comedy*, p. 95.
36. Ibid., p. 109.
37. MacDonald, *Don't Touch*, p. 126.
38. Wertheim, *Radio Comedy*, p. 68.
39. Ibid., p. 80.
40. MacDonald, *Don't Touch*, p. 43.
41. Ibid., p. 155.
42. Ibid., pp. 160–74.
43. Ibid., pp. 234–48.
44. Ibid., p. 248.
45. Erik Barnouw, *The Golden Web: A History of Broadcasting in the United States* (New York: Oxford University Press, 1968), vol. II, pp. 18–22.
46. MacDonald, *Don't Touch*, p. 298.
47. Irving Fang, *Those Radio Commentators* (Ames: Iowa State University Press, 1977), pp. 6–7, 107–11.
48. Elisha Hanson, "Official Propaganda and the New Deal." *Annals of the American Academy of Political and Social Science* 179 (5–1935), p. 185.
49. MacDonald, *Don't Touch*, pp. 288–89.
50. Editor and Publisher, 7–13–1940.
51. Stearns, *America Now*, p. 12.
52. MacDonald, *Don't Touch*, pp. 47–48.
53. Ibid., p. 48.
54. Ibid., pp. 51–54.
55. Ibid., pp. 54–55.
56. Quoted in Foster R. Dulles, *America Learns to Play* (New York: Appleton-Century, 1965), p. 335.
57. Ibid.
58. Barnouw, *Golden Web*, pp. 40–42, 129–30.
59. Ibid., pp. 38, 126.

CHAPTER FIVE

1. Deems Taylor, "Music," in Harold E. Stearns, ed., *America Now* (New York: Scribner's, 1938), p. 65.
2. Barry Ulanov, *A History of Jazz in America* (New York: Viking, 1957), pp. 156–57.
3. D. Duane Braun, *The Sociology and History of American Music and Dance* (Ann Arbor, MI: Ann Arbor Publishers, 1969), pp. 26–27.
4. Paul Sann, *Fads, Follies and Delusions of the American People* (New York: Crown, 1938), pp. 347–48.
5. Ulanov, *Jazz*, pp. 158–59.
6. Sann, *Fads, Follies*, p. 349.
7. Marshall W. Stearns, *The Story of Jazz* (New York: Oxford University Press, 1956), p. 189.
8. Ulanov, *Jazz*, pp. 184–85.

9. Stearns, *Story of Jazz*, p. 198.

10. Ibid., p. 209–11.

11. Ulanov, *Jazz*, p. 194.

12. Frederick Lewis Allen, *Since Yesterday* (New York: Bantam Books, 1965), p. 214.

13. Braun, *Music and Dance*, pp. 48–50.

14. New York *Herald-Tribune*, 10–12–1938.

15. Allen, *Since Yesterday*, pp. 216–17.

16. *The New Republic*, 10–5–1938, p. 34.

17. *The Saturday Evening Post*, 1–28–1939.

18. *Newsweek*, 6–3–1940, p. 48.

19. Ibid.

20. Tom Murray, "You Pay Before You Play," *Nation's Business*, 6–1940, p. 30.

21. Allen, *Since Yesterday*, p. 222.

22. Reid, in Stearns, *America Now*, p. 23.

23. Maxine Davis, *The Lost Generation* (New York: Macmillan, 1936), pp. 133–35.

24. Dixon Wecter, *The Age of the Great Depression, 1929–1941* (New York: Macmillan, 1948), p. 237.

25. Malcom M. Willey and Stuart A. Rice, *Communication Agencies and Social Life* (New York: McGraw-Hill, 1933), p. 182.

26. Foster R. Dulles, *America Learns to Play* (New York: Appleton-Century, 1965), pp. 302–3.

27. New York *Herald-Tribune*, 3–27–1934.

28. *Fortune*, 12–1935, p. 7.

29. Allen, *Since Yesterday*, pp. 223–24.

30. Lewis Jacobs, *The Rise of the American Film* (New York: Teachers College Press, 1967), p. 517.

31. New York *Herald-Tribune*, 3–27–1934.

32. Reid, in Stearns, *America Now*, p. 24.

33. *United States News*, 12–4–1933.

34. Paul Mallon in Omaha *World-Herald*, 10–5–1936.

35. Quoted in Robert Heide and John Gilman, *Dime-Store Dream Parade* (New York: Dutton, 1979), p. 108.

36. Jacobs, *American Film* p. 519.

37. Reid, in Stearns, *America Now*, p. 35.

38. Willey and Rice, *Communication Agencies*, p. 183.

39. *Time*, 2–3–1936, p. 57.

40. Forbes Parkhill, in *The Saturday Evening Post*, 12–4–1937, p. 20.

41. *Time*, 2–3–1936, p. 57.

42. Dulles, *America Learns to Play*, pp. 306–8.

43. Holger Cahill, "American Art Today," in Fred J. Ringel, ed., *America as Americans See It* (New York: Harcourt, Brace, 1932), p. 258.

44. Martha C. Cheney, *Modern Art in America* (New York: McGraw-Hill, 1939), p. 121.

45. Quoted in ibid., p. 123.

46. Quoted in ibid.

47. Lowell Thompson, "America's Day Dream," *Saturday Review* 11–13–1937, p. 16.

48. Cheney, *Modern Art*, p. 127.

49. Ibid., pp. 139–50.

50. Lloyd Goodrich, "Painting and Sculpture," in Robert E. Spiller and Eric Larrabee, eds., *American Perspectives* (Cambridge, MA: Harvard University Press, 1961), p. 84.

51. Alice G. Marquis, *Hopes and Ashes*, New York: Free Press, 1986), pp. 163–64.

52. Cheney, *Modern Art*, p. 164.

53. Goodrich, in Spiller and Larrabee, *American Perspectives*, pp. 83–84.

54. William P. Randel, *The Evolution of American Taste* (New York: Crown, 1978), pp. 174–75.

55. Heide and Gilman, *Dime Store*, p. 17.

56. *Editor and Publisher*, 2–2–1935.

CHAPTER SIX

1. John R. Tunis, "The Business of American Sports," in Fred J. Ringel, ed., *America as Americans See It* (New York: Harcourt, Brace, 1937), p. 119.

2. *Literary Digest*, 10–21–1933, p. 10.

3. Washington *Post*, 11–17–1935.

4. New York *Times*, 11–30–1938.

5. For details on college football during the 1930s I have relied mainly on Allison Danzig, *The History of American Football* (Englewood Cliffs, NJ: Prentice-Hall, 1956), pp. 305–57.

6. *Literary Digest*, 7–16–1932, pp. 32–33.

7. H. I. Phillips, "Hold 'em Mike!" *The Saturday Evening Post*, 10–17–1936, pp. 25, 95.

8. New York *Times*, 6–26–1939; Pegler in Omaha *World-Herald*, 6–21–1933.

9. Chicago *Tribune*, 3–23–1933.

10. *Editor and Publisher*, 3–2–1935.

11. Allison Danzig and Joe Reichler, *The History of Baseball* (Englewood Cliffs, NJ: Prentice-Hall, 1959), p. 81.

12. Harold Claassen, *The History of Professional Football* (Englewood Cliffs, NJ: Prentice-Hall, 1963), p. 69.

13. Quoted in Benjamin G. Rader, *American Sports* (Englewood Cliffs, NJ: Prentice-Hall, 1983), p. 253.

14. John D. McCallum, *College Basketball, U.S.A.* (New York: Stein and Day, 1978), p. 51.

15. Ibid., pp. 54–61.

16. Frederick Lewis Allen, *Since Yesterday* (New York: Bantam Books, 1965), p. 27.

17. Herbert W. Wind, *The Story of American Golf* (Westport, CT: Greenwood, 1972), p. 295.

18. Ibid., p. 297.

19. Paul Gallico, "The Texas Babe," reprinted from *Vanity Fair* in Don Congdon, *The Thirties* (New York: Simon & Schuster, 1962), pp. 73–74.

20. *Time*, 9–16–1935, p. 47.
21. Allen, *Since Yesterday*, p. 120.
22. Ibid., p. 121.

CHAPTER SEVEN

1. Newman Levy, "The Sartorial Revolution," *Harper's*, 6–1936, pp. 100, 102.
2. Chicago *Tribune*, 6–29–1936.
3. Pitkin, in Fred J. Ringel, ed., *America as Americans See It* (New York: Harcourt, Brace, 1932), p. 203.
4. Ibid.
5. Paul Sann, *Fads, Follies and Delusions of the American People* (New York: Crown, 1967), pp. 265–66.
6. Malcolm M. Willey and Stuart A. Rice, *Communication Agencies and Social Life* (New York: McGraw-Hill, 1933), p. 182.
7. Maxine Davis, *The Lost Generation* (New York: Macmillan, 1936), p. 136.
8. Dorothy D. Bromley and Florence H. Britten, *Youth and Sex* (New York: Harper, 1938), pp. 16–17.
9. Ibid., pp. 29–30.
10. Washington *Post*, 8–24–1934.
11. Robert S. Lynd and Helen M. Lynd, *Middletown in Transition* (New York: Harcourt, Brace, 1937), pp. 10, 265–66.
12. Foster R. Dulles, *America Learns to Play* (New York: Appleton-Century, 1965), p. 319.
13. Corey Ford, "How to Solve the Traffic Situation," in Don Congdon, ed., *The Thirties* (New York: Simon & Schuster, 1967), p. 34.
14. Bernard DeVoto, "The Consumer's Automobile," *Harper's*, 5–1936, p. 718.
15. Dulles, *America Learns to Play*, p. 318.
16. U.S. Department of Commerce, Bureau of the Census, *Historical Statistics of the United States*, Vol. I (Washington, DC: Government Printing Office, 1975), 396.
17. Ibid., p. 396.
18. Dulles, *America Learns to Play*, p. 320.
19. Robert Heide and John Gilman, *Dime-Store Dream Parade* (New York: Dutton, 1979), p. 95.
20. Douglas Haskell, "Architecture," in Harold E. Stearns, ed., *America Now* (New York: Scribner's, 1938), pp. 110–11.
21. Willey and Rice, *Communication Agencies*, pp. 66–67.
22. Ibid., p. 67.
23. Pitkin, in Ringel, *America as Americans See It*, p. 202.
24. Elmer Daves, in ibid., p. 213.
25. Ibid., pp. 78–87.
26. *Newsweek*, 3–7–1936, p. 36.
27. *Literary Digest*, 8–22–1936, p. 16.
28. *Newsweek*, 3–7–1936, p. 36.
29. Tom Murray, "You Pay Before You Play," *Nation's Business*, 6–1940, p. 28.
30. Dixon Wecter, *The Age of the Great Depression 1929–1941* (New York: Macmillan, 1948), p. 226.

31. Frederick Lewis Allen, *Since Yesterday* (New York: Bantam Books, 1965), p. 184.

32. *Saturday Review*, 8-7-1937, p. 10.

33. Dulles, *America Learns to Play*, p. 321.

34. Wecter, *Great Depression*, pp. 226-27.

35. Haskell, in Stearns, *America Now*, pp. 113-14.

36. Allen, *Since Yesterday*, p. 105.

37. Arthur Gleason, "Distorted Standards," *Catholic World*, 2-1935, pp. 577-80.

38. Davis, *Lost Generation*, p. 76.

39. Quoted in Omaha *World-Herald*, 4-18-1936.

40. Davis, *Lost Generation*, pp. 4-5.

41. Quoted in ibid., p. 10.

42. Bromley and Britten, *Youth and Sex*, p. 4.

43. Ibid., pp. 11-12.

44. Ibid., pp. 240-46.

45. Hannah M. Stone, "Birth Rate and Population, in Stearns, *America Now*, pp. 458-61; Wecter, *Great Depression*, pp. 178-80.

46. Bromley and Britten, *Youth and Sex*, p. 5.

47. Ibid., pp. 258-59.

48. Davis, *Lost Generation*, p. 83.

49. Bromley and Britten, *Youth and Sex*, p. 13.

50. Stone, in Stearns, *America Now*, pp. 458-61; Wecter, *Great Depression*, pp. 178-80.

51. Gleason, "Distorted Standards," p. 579.

52. Bromley and Britten, *Youth and Sex*, pp. 13-14.

53. Wecter, *Great Depression*, p. 179.

54. Ibid., pp. 185-86.

55. Thacher Winslow, "Youth in Crisis," in Thacher Winslow and Frank P. Davidson, eds., *American Youth: An Enforced Reconnaissance* (Cambridge, MA: Harvard University Press, 1940), pp. 43-47.

56. Wecter, *Great Depression*, pp. 185-86.

57. Ibid., pp. 187-88, 193.

58. Winslow, "Youth in Crisis," p. 49.

59. Wecter, *Great Depression*, pp. 195-96.

60. Ibid., pp. 198-200.

61. Ibid., pp. 212-14.

62. Allen, *Since Yesterday*, pp. 127-28.

CHAPTER EIGHT

1. Summarized in Dixon Wecter, *The Age of the Great Depression, 1929-1941* (New York: Macmillan, 1948), pp. 272-73.

2. Advertisement in Chicago *Tribune*, 6-5-1936; *Editor and Publisher*, 2-29-1936.

3. Pitkin, in Fred J. Ringel, ed., *America as Americans See It* (New York: Harcourt, Brace, 1932), p. 203.

4. Omaha *World-Herald*, 3-4-1933.

5. Robert S. Lynd and Helen M. Lynd, *Middletown in Transition* (New York: Harcourt, Brace, 1937), pp. 10–11.

6. Ibid., p. 20.

7. Ibid., pp. 250–51.

8. Ibid., p. 76.

9. Ibid., p. 105.

10. C. R. Fellers, "Foods and the Economic Crisis," *American Journal of Public Health*, 2–1935, pp. 58–61.

11. "Gardening for Relief," *Review of Reviews*, 5–1933, p. 42; "Relief Gardens," *The Survey*, 4–1934, p. 134.

12. All quoted in Mirra Komarovsky, *The Unemployed Man and His Family*, p. 123.

13. Ibid., pp. 124–25.

14. Ibid., p. 127.

CONCLUSION

1. Frederick W. Marks III, *Wind Over Sand* (Athens: University of Georgia Press, 1988), p. 260.

2. Bernard DeVoto, "Memento for New Year's Day," *Harper's*, 1–1936, p. 253.

3. Lowell Thompson, "America's Day Dream," *Saturday Review*, 11–13–1937, p. 16.

4. Gene Smith, *The Shattered Dream: Herbert Hoover and the Great Depression* (New York: Morrow, 1970), p. 67.

Bibliography

MANUSCRIPT COLLECTIONS

Thomas W. Lamont Papers, Baker Library, Harvard University.
Amos Pinchot Papers, Library of Congress.
Mark Sullivan Papers, Library of Congress.

NEWSPAPERS

Chicago *Tribune*
New York *Herald-Tribune*
New York *Times*
Omaha *World-Herald*
Washington *Post*

MAJOR MAGAZINES AND JOURNALS

American Mercury
Business Week
Commercial and Financial Chronicle
The Economist
Editor and Publisher
Forbes
Literary Digest

The Nation

Nation's Business

The New Republic

Newsweek

The Saturday Evening Post

Saturday Review

Scientific American

Time

United States News

BOOKS

Allen, Frederick Lewis. *Since Yesterday*. New York: Bantam Books, 1965.
Baldwin, Hanson W., and Shepard Stone, eds. *We Saw it Happen*. New York: Simon & Schuster, 1938.
Barnouw, Erik. *The Golden Web: A History of Broadcasting in the United States*. New York: Oxford University Press, 1968.
Best, Gary Dean. *The Critical Press and the New Deal: The Press versus Presidential Power, 1933–1938*. Westport, CT: Praeger, 1993.
———. *Pride, Prejudice and Politics: Roosevelt versus Recovery 1933–1938*. New York: Praeger, 1991.
Braun, D. Duane. *The Sociology and History of American Music and Dance*. Ann Arbor, MI: Ann Arbor Publishers, 1969.
Bromley, Dorothy D., and Florence H. Britten. *Youth and Sex*. New York: Harper's, 1938.
Cavan, Ruth S., and Katherine H. Ranck. *The Family and The Depression*. Chicago: University of Chicago Press, 1938.
Cheney, Martha C. *Modern Art in America*. New York: McGraw-Hill, 1939.
Claassen, Harold. *The History of Professional Football*. Englewood Cliffs, NJ: Prentice-Hall, 1963.
Congdon, Don, ed. *The Thirties*. New York: Simon & Schuster, 1962.
Danzig, Allison. *The History of American Football*. Englewood Cliffs, NJ: Prentice-Hall, 1956.
———, and Joe Reichler. *The History of Baseball*. Englewood Cliffs, NJ: Prentice-Hall, 1959.
Davis, Maxine. *The Lost Generation*. New York: Macmillan, 1936.
Dulles, Foster R. *America Learns to Play*. New York: Appleton-Century, 1965.
Emery, Edwin. *The Press and America*. Englewood Cliffs, NJ: Prentice-Hall, 1972.
Fang, Irving. *Those Radio Commentators*. Ames: Iowa State University Press, 1977.
Feather, Norman T. *The Psychological Impact of Unemployment*. New York: Springer-Verlag, 1990.
Halliday, Jon, and Peter Fuller, eds., *The Psychology of Gambling*. New York: Harper & Row, 1974.
Hayes, John, and Peter Nutman. *Understanding the Unemployed: The Psychological Effects of Unemployment*. London: Tavistock, 1981.

Hearn, Charles R. *The American Dream in the Great Depression*. Westport, CT: Greenwood, 1977.

Heide, Robert, and John Gilman. *Dime-Store Dream Parade*. New York: Dutton, 1979.

Inge, M. Thomas, ed. *Handbook of American Popular Literature*. Westport, CT: Greenwood, 1988.

Jacobs, Lewis. *The Rise of the American Film*. New York: Teachers College Press, 1967.

Kelvin, Peter, and Joanna E. Jarrett. *Unemployment: Its Social Psychological Effects*. New York: Cambridge University Press, 1985.

Komarovsky, Mirra. *The Unemployed Man and His Family*. New York: Dryden, 1940.

Laughlin, H. P. *The Ego and Its Defenses*. New York: J. Aronson, 1979.

Lynd, Robert S., and Helen M. Lynd. *Middletown in Transition*. New York: Harcourt, Brace, 1937.

MacDonald, J. Fred. *Don't Touch That Dial: Radio Programming in American Life from 1920 to 1960*. Chicago: Nelson-Hall, 1979.

Madden, David, ed. *Tough Guy Writers of the Thirties*. Carbondale: Southern Illinois University Press, 1968.

Marks, Frederick W. III. *Wind Over Sand*. Athens: University of Georgia Press, 1988.

Marquis, Alice G. *Hopes and Ashes*. New York: Free Press, 1986.

McCallum, John D. *College Basketball, U.S.A.* New York: Stein and Day, 1978.

McCamy, James L. *Government Publicity: Its Practice in Federal Administration*. Chicago: University of Chicago Press, 1939.

McIntire, Vice Admiral Ross T. *White House Physician*. New York: Putnam's, 1946.

Mott, Frank Luther. *American Journalism*. New York: Macmillan, 1962.

Peterson, Theodore B. *Magazines in the Twentieth Century*. Urbana: University of Illinois Press, 1956.

Philips, Cabell, ed. *Dateline: Washington*. Garden City, NY: Doubleday, 1949.

Rader, Benjamin G. *American Sports*. Englewood Cliffs, NJ: Prentice-Hall, 1983.

Randel, William P. *The Evolution of American Taste*. New York: Crown, 1978.

Ringel, Fred J., ed. *America as Americans See It*. New York: Harcourt, Brace, 1932.

Roper, Daniel. *Fifty Years of Public Life*. Durham, NC: Duke University Press, 1941.

Rosten, Leo C. *The Washington Correspondents*. New York: Harcourt, Brace, 1974 (reprint of 1937 edition).

Sann, Paul. *Fads, Follies and Delusions of the American People*. New York: Crown, 1967.

Smith, Gene. *The Shattered Dream: Herbert Hoover and the Great Depression*. New York: Morrow, 1970.

Spiller, Robert E., and Eric Larrabee, eds. *American Perspectives*. Cambridge, MA: Harvard University Press, 1961.

Stearns, Harold E., ed. *America Now*. New York: Scribner's, 1938.

Stearns, Marshall W. *The Story of Jazz*. New York: Oxford University Press, 1956.

Ulanov, Barry. *A History of Jazz in America*. New York: Viking, 1957.

U.S. Department of Commerce, Bureau of the Census. *Historical Statistics of the United States*. Two volumes. Washington, DC: Government Printing Office, 1975.

Watts, Emily S. *The Businessman in American Literature*. Athens: University of Georgia Press, 1982.

Wecter, Dixon. *The Age of the Great Depression, 1929–1941*. New York: Macmillan, 1948.

Wertheim, Arthur F. *Radio Comedy*. New York: Oxford University Press, 1979.

Willey, Malcom M., and Stuart A. Rice. *Communication Agencies and Social Life*. New York: McGraw-Hill, 1933.

Wind, Herbert W. *The Story of American Golf*. Westport, CT: Greenwood, 1972.

Winslow, Thacher, and Frank P. Davidson, eds. *American Youth: An Enforced Reconnaissance*. Cambridge, MA: Harvard University Press, 1940.

Wood, James P. *Magazines in the United States*. New York: Ronald, 1956.

Zastrow, Charles, and Karen Kirst-Ashman. *Understanding Human Behavior and the Social Environment*. Chicago: Nelson-Hall, 1987.

ARTICLES

Berchtold, William E. "Press Agents of the New Deal." *New Outlook*, 7–26–1934.

"Brother, Can You Spare a Dime?" *New Republic*, 5–22–1935.

"Camera Action." *Business Week*, 1–5–1935.

Copeland, George H. "The Country Is Off on a Jig-Saw Jag." New York *Times Magazine*, 2–12–1933.

Crichton, K. "Jam in the Saucer." *Collier's*, 2–23–1935.

"Dance Marathoners." *The Survey*, 2–1934.

DeVoto, Bernard. "Memento for New Year's Day," *Harper's*, 1–1936.

———. "The Consumer's Automobile." *Harper's* 5–1936.

"Does the World Owe Me a Living?" *Scribner's Magazine*, 5–1934.

Eisenberg, P., and P. F. Lazarsfeld. "The Psychological Effects of Unemployment." *Psychological Bulletin*, 35 (1938).

Fellers, C. R. "Foods and the Economic Crisis." *American Journal of Public Health*, 2–1935.

"Gardening for Relief." *Review of Reviews*, 5–1933.

Gleason, Arthur. "Distorted Standards." *Catholic World*, 2–1935.

Hanson, Elisha. "Official Propaganda and the New Deal." *Annals of the American Academy of Political and Social Science* 179 (5–1935).

"Hooverism in the Funnies." *New Republic*, 7–11–1934.

Kennedy, J. B. "Good-Night Lady: Marathon Dancing." *Collier's*, 7–23–1932.

Le Sueur, Meridel. "The Sleepwalkers." *The New Republic*, 2–2–1933.

Levick, M. B. "Games and Puzzles Gain." New York *Times*, 4–14–1935.

Levy, Newman. "The Sartorial Revolution." *Harper's*, 6–1936.

Lubell, Samuel. "Ten Billion Nickels." *The Saturday Evening Post*, 5–13–1939.

Murray, Tom. "You Pay Before You Play." *Nation's Business*, 6–1940.

Nock, Albert Jay. "The Amazing Liberal Mind." *American Mercury*, 8–1938.

"1,500,000 Dry Shavers . . . ." *Fortune*, 5–1938.

Payne, Will. "The New Prohibition." *The Saturday Evening Post*, 8–19–1933.

Phillips, H. I. "Hold 'em Mike!" *The Saturday Evening Post*, 10–17–1936.

Reeves, C. B. "Brief for the Bankers." *American Mercury*, 9–32.

"Relief Gardens." *The Survey*, 4–1934.

Reynolds, Quentin. "Round & Round." *Collier's*, 8–22–1936.

Rice, J.A.G. "Play's the Thing." *The Saturday Evening Post*, 4–7–1934.
Sokolsky, George. "The Psychology of the New Deal." *Atlantic Monthly*, 3–1936.
"Sport in the Nickel Age." *Business Week*, 3–29–1933.
Sprague, Marshall. "New Games for Indoors." New York *Times*, 11–29–1936.
Thompson, Lowell. "America's Day-Dream." *Saturday Review*, 11–13–1937.
Wharton, Don. "Commentators." *Today*, 5–30–1936.

Index

ABOUT THE AUTHOR

GARY DEAN BEST is Professor of History at the University of Hawaii at Hilo. He is the author of *The Politics of American Individualism* (Greenwood, 1975), *To Free a People* (Greenwood, 1982), *Herbert Hoover: The Postpresidential Years* (2 volumes, 1983), *Pride, Prejudice, and Politics: Roosevelt versus Recovery, 1933–1938* (Praeger, 1991), *FDR and the Bonus Marchers, 1933–1935* (Praeger, 1992), and *The Critical Press and the New Deal: The Press versus Presidential Power, 1933–1938* (Praeger, 1993), as well as numerous essays for scholarly books and journals. He has held fellowships from the American Historical Association and the National Endowment for the Humanities and was a Fulbright Scholar in Japan from 1974 to 1975.